The Histo
Widecomb

ORCHARD PUBLICATIONS
2 Orchard Close, Chudleigh, Devon TQ13 0LR
Telephone: (01626) 852714

ISBN 9781898964797

Printed by
Hedgerow Print, Crediton, Devon EX17 1ES

i

CONTENTS

Acknowledgements
The Widecombe and District Local History Group would like to acknowledge all the help given to them from various sources, far too many to mention individually, for photographs, documents and information shared in the production of this book. Special mention must be made of *The Western Morning News, Mid-Devon Advertiser, Express & Echo* and other local newspapers for their kind permission to use extracts from their publications. We would also like to thank the Roach family from Crediton and the Brook family from Spreyton, both descendant from Tom Cobley, for their support with our research.

INTRODUCTION

There are many stories attributed to Widecombe Fair, how it began and when, so let us put them all together and call this a **Pocket History of a Great Day Out.** For many hundreds of years, Fairs have been held across the country at various times of the year. These Fairs had a very important part to play in the agricultural year as well as being a social event. It was a time to review the harvest, calculate whether there was enough food to carry their stock through the coming winter and, if not, to adjust their stocking levels accordingly. These Autumn Fairs were also an opportunity to reduce or increase the stock, exchange rams and bulls to perpetuate their stock rearing, sell off surplus breeding ewes, store wether lambs, store cattle and older cows that would be bought by the farmers of the lower lands to breed from or fatten up for slaughter.

Widecombe Fair on the Green, early 20th Century

It is generally accepted that a sheep, cattle and pony Fair has been part of the Widecombe calendar for many decades. However, the earliest written record of Widecombe Fair found so far appears to be a report in the Woolman's *Exeter and Plymouth Gazette* dated Saturday, 19th October 1850, being an announcement that 'on the following Friday, 25th October 1850, a Free Fair would be held on the Green adjoining the Church Yard at Widecombe-in-the Moor. There would be a large Show of cattle and a quantity of moorland sheep offered for sale'. A fortnight later, on Saturday, 2nd November 1850, the *Gazette* reported

The traditional 'old grey mare' whose type the song imortalises, passing down the village street to the famous Widecombe Fair.

that 'A Cattle Fair was held at Widecombe-in-the-Moor for the first time on Tuesday last, 29th October 1850. There was a large attendance of yeomen and gentlemen of the district and good business was done. It was thought that the Fair should be permanently established. 736 sheep were penned, 75 store and 7 fatted beasts were sold plus 4 bulls. One South Devon cow, reared by the Vicar Reverend J. H. Mason, was sold for £15.10s.0d. About 50 ponies were driven in, the breed and character of the Widecombe stock being highly appreciated. It was intended to fix the future date not to clash with any neighbouring fair. It was agreed that Widecombe was fortunate to have a Green that was an ideal spot to hold a Free Fair.'

The Vicar, well known for his hospitality, held a large dinner party and celebrated the Fair in 'Fine Old English Style'. Mr. John Germon of Moreton presided and it is said that the guests left 'brimful of enjoyment.'

From the Parish Register the guests included:

John Tozer of Solomon Tozer, Agent for the Rev. T. Fry.

Lord of the Manor of Widecombe.

Thomas Escot, Cresswell.

John Germon, Moretonhampstead, Chairman.

James Woodley, Halshanger - brought 34 sheep.

John Sparke Amay (Amery), Druid, Ashburton.

William White, Solicitor, Moretonhampstead.

Wm. A. Cockley, Solicitor, Ashburton.
H.C. Creagh, Surveyor, Ashburton.
Robt. Nosworthy, Ford, Manaton.
Henry Hals, Scagell, Farmer.
John May, Yeoman, Moretonhampstead
W.B. Germon, Yeoman, Morton.
John Pearse, Butcher, Ashburton.
John Coaker, Yeoman, Bellaford.

Widecombe Fair is now always held on the second Tuesday of September, so it can therefore fluctuate between the 8th and the 14th of the month, but whichever date it falls on, the locals always consider winter starts on the very next day. The local farmers liked to have completed their harvest by Fair day, so they could let their hair down as the year's work was completed and prepare for entry into the autumn and winter months.

It is generally agreed that the characters in the song came from mid-Devon. There was a Thomas Cobley who died in Spreyton in 1794. His great nephew, a Thomas Cobley of Butsford in the Parish of Colebrook, died in 1844 aged 82 years and is buried at Spreyton, just outside the south door of the Church.

Uncle Tom Cobley's signature on his Will

3

CERTIFIED COPY OF AN ENTRY OF DEATH

GIVEN AT THE **GENERAL REGISTER OFFICE**

Application Number PAS1076970

REGISTRATION DISTRICT					Crediton			
1844 DEATH in the Sub-district of Crediton					in the County of Devon			

Columns:–	1	2	3	4	5	6	7	8	9
No.	When and where died	Name and surname	Sex	Age	Occupation	Cause of death	Signature, description and residence of informant	When registered	Signature of registrar
357	Fifth of January 1844 at Colebrook	Thomas Cobley	Male	82 years	Yeoman	Debility	The Mark of Elizabeth Jackson Present at the Death Colebrook	Ninth of January 1844	Edward Yande Registrar

CERTIFIED to be a true copy of an entry in the certified copy of a Register of Deaths in the District above mentioned.

Given at the GENERAL REGISTER OFFICE, under the Seal of the said Office, the .... 24th .... day of .... November 2005

DYA 835200

See note overleaf

CAUTION: THERE ARE OFFENCES RELATING TO FALSIFYING OR ALTERING A CERTIFICATE AND USING OR POSSESSING A FALSE CERTIFICATE ©CROWN COPYRIGHT
WARNING: A CERTIFICATE IS NOT EVIDENCE OF IDENTITY.

TW

Thomas Cobley's Death Certificate 1844

The Tavern sign at Spreyton.

This gentleman is thought to be the character in the song by the present day descendents of the Cobley family. This conclusion would fit well with the name board on the Tom Cobley Tavern at Spreyton which states that Uncle Tom Cobley left there to go to Widecombe Fair in 1802. It is probable that the present day Tom Cobley Tavern was then known as the White Hart.

Tom Cobley's companions, Bill Brewer, Jan Stewer, etc, are reputed to have lived in Sticklepath but the names vary with the different versions of the song. The Brewers, Stewers, Gurneys, Whiddons, Davys and Pearses can certainly be found in old papers relating to mid-Devon. Could it be that it was the norm to use the names of local characters in the song for particular local amusement?

The Widecombe Fair Committee minute books from 1923 to the present day have been made available while writing this book and, through reading them, and other material such as newspaper cuttings, a very interesting picture of the Fair's history has been built up.

Research has demonstrated much inconsistency in the spellings of names:

- *Widecombe* also appears as *Widdecombe*, *Widdicombe*, *Withycombe* and even *Widlicombe*.

- *Cobley* and *Cobleigh* are both commonly used.

- *Pearse* can be found as *Pearce* and *Pierce*.

A LOOK AT MARKETS AND FAIRS

To appreciate the importance of markets and fairs to the rural life, we need to go back to the beginning of agricultural activity over the last 2000 years. Once man decided to domesticate animals, there was a need to control their breeding. In the wild, animals practice their own selection, generally by the survival of the strongest, or by the dominant male controlling more than his share of the females at his disposal. Natural predation also meant that the strongest survived while the weakest fell prey to their predators, sickness or injury. There was much injury caused by the action of fighting for precedent, all leading to natural selection.

At the time when man was a hunter, he too selected the weakest animals and the easiest to capture and kill. It can be said that this is the principal of any form of hunting, be it by man or animal. Once the animals were being herded and in constant control of man, selective breeding began. It was found that one male could be used to service several females and the poorer quality males were culled for meat while the better ones were kept as breeding sires. By keeping groups of animals in seclusion from others, it would be easy to get inbreeding, where in the wild they scatter and their genes would get distributed.

Gradually the farmer/gatherer would appreciate this and recognise the possibility that another man had an animal that he would like. By bartering, a process of exchange of stock would develop. This would have been the origin of trading. As this practice increased, certain places on certain days of the year were found to be ideal for these transactions. As conventional religion took over from pagan practices, certain Saints' days became the normal days for such gatherings. This was the beginning of Fairs or Markets and many today are still held on Saint Days, some with names alluding to the Saint concerned. St Michael brings to mind Michaelmas Day (29th September), the feast day of St Michael and All Angels.

Mosaic presented to Widecombe History Group by David Cocker, aged 15

Several fairs were created by Charters issued by Royal Decree; there are good examples dating from over a thousand years ago. Here in Devon there are Charter Fairs at Barnstaple and Chulmleigh, both having the symbol of a glove in their proclamation, denoting Royal Approval. This type of Fair gradually incorporated gypsies, fairgrounds and fête-like stalls and celebrations.

Gypsies at the Fair by Pamela Coleman Smith

Agriculture is controlled by the environment in which it is practised. To understand the farming practices of years gone by will help to understand how and why certain events developed and were so important to the rural community of that time.

Most farmers were tenant farmers. Landowners, as the name suggests, owned the land. This included farms, cottages, woodland and in many cases the open moorland as well. It was a feudal system. The landowners and the church were all powerful and they were intertwined to a great degree. In many cases the Squire (Lord of the Manor) was the main benefactor to the church and its incumbent often one of his sons.

The tenant farmer had a very strict agreement with his landlord; in many cases the agreement stipulated what had to be done each year and when. If this was not strictly adhered to, the tenant could easily be given notice to quit. The agricultural worker generally lived in a 'tied cottage', that is a cottage belonging to the farm, and he too had to obey without question the demands of his employer and especially not do anything that would upset the landlord. He could be out of house, home and work at a minute's notice. It can be seen from this that the 'hierarchy' by its very name were all powerful.

In normal circumstances, agricultural tenancies began and ended on one of the four quarter days. Lady Day (25th March), Mid-Summer Day (24th June), Michaelmas Day (29th September) and Christmas Day (25th December). The two principal ones were Lady Day and Michaelmas Day. Why was this? To change in the middle of summer or winter would be impractical for several reasons. At mid-summer all the crops would be sown and growing. Hay harvest would have been in full swing, corn harvest would be six weeks away, swedes would have only just been sown and all the other crops like mangolds, flatpole cabbages, potatoes and kale would be only half way through their growing season. The animals would be out to grass, the ewes with their lambs and the cows with their calves. On Dartmoor many of these animals would be out on the moors exercising the Commoners' rights. At Christmas the cows would be in shippons by night and the store cattle (those twelve months and older) would winter outdoors, being fed on hay and straw. The sheep would have been 'in lamb' ready for lambing in the coming March and, with the last year's ewe lambs that were being kept for replacements, many would be off Dartmoor for six or eight weeks eating swedes down on 'incountry farms'. To have a sale and move farm at any other time of the year than March or September would be totally impractical.

Two farmers and Beatrice Chase admiring the sheep

At Lady Day the farmer would be looking forward to spring and most of his hay and straw would be used up. A small amount of his root crops would still be available to him and his stock would be at its lowest number. With the coming of spring, the cows would begin to calve and the sheep to lamb, and total stock numbers would increase. At Michaelmas the bulk of his harvest would have been completed. The crops in the fields would be fully matured and the moorland farmer would be able to work out how well he would be able to cope with the coming winter. He would know whether he had enough fodder to take his stock through the winter months. If he decided that he did not, he could sell off the surplus cattle and sheep. This is where the annual cattle and sheep fairs/ markets came into their own. There was one other very important decision facing him. Could he pay the rent? The rent was generally due twice a year, at Lady Day and Michaelmas. All these factors helped to develop the market and fair system.

A fair in March enabled the farmer to sell some cattle and get some cash to settle firstly his rent and secondly any bills that had accumulated during the winter months. It was a common sight to see representatives of the cattle food and seed suppliers at these markets and business being transacted. At some of these markets the suppliers even had their own wooden huts, where they stood waiting for their customers and, in due course, agricultural machinery suppliers also came onto the scene.

Judging Widecombe Whitefaced Dartmoor Sheep

Michaelmas fairs were the means of selling surplus stock that moorland farmers, in particular, felt that they could not feed through the coming winter. Cattle from the poorer areas of Dartmoor were always in demand as they could be guaranteed to improve (do well) when brought in to the more productive and fertile lands off the moors. Breeding stock was also sold at this time including breeding ewes, particularly the Widecombe Whitefaced Dartmoor sheep. Surplus 'store' cattle (mainly South Devon breed) and lambs were also sold and the autumn sales were well attended, a great deal of business being transacted.

If we cast our attention back to the beginning of these fairs, we find that the normal way of business was a system of bartering. If Farmer A wanted to do a deal with Farmer B they would argue over which had the best ram, pen of ewes, cow, bull or horse, and the final 'slap of hands' would settle the deal, resulting in an exchange of stock and possibly a small amount of money. This continued for generations, until gradually a system of auctions crept into these fairs, where individuals could bid against one another to acquire the stock on offer. The fairs were known to be the best opportunity for farmers and dealers to meet and do business. It is worth pointing out that farmers attended several fairs over the course of the agricultural year. After the business of the day was transacted, they would retire to the local hostelry for some much needed social contact.

It is apparent that Widecombe Fair was one of these important annual events, just one of thousands around the country. In the early days they served the local area with farmers and dealers perhaps travelling no more than thirty or forty miles to attend. Drovers were on hire to drive the stock to and from the fairs. Gradually over the past one hundred and fifty years, with the coming of the railways and road transport, buyers and sellers alike travelled farther afield to buy and sell their wares. Looking at Dartmoor, places like Princetown, Ashburton, Moretonhampstead, Okehampton, Dousland, Tavistock and South Brent had a railway and markets grew up nearby.

Trains with many cattle trucks would be brought to these places ready for the fairs, and the stock would be sent all over the country. With the demise of these branch railways some of these small but excellent markets died out. With road improvements and larger cattle lorries, road transport became more popular and therefore expanded markets in Market Towns. Since the dreadful foot and mouth disease outbreak of 2001, many of these too have disappeared or reduced in size, partly due to direct marketing between farmers and abattoirs.

Widecombe-in-the-Moor was one the venues for an annual fair, a place where cattle, sheep and ponies were sold. The indigenous Dartmoor Pony reared on the high moors around the valley was one type of stock sold here. This hardy strong breed of pony had many uses – riding, carriage work, light work on farms and the really unfortunate ones ended their lives as pit ponies in coal mines. The South Devon cattle, a hardy productive animal bred in the area, good for milk and beef, were always in demand, for the incountry farmer to purchase and rear for breeding or to fatten for slaughter. It was a dual purpose animal producing good quality beef and milk at 4% butterfat, ideal for the production of the traditional Devonshire clotted (clouted) cream. The Widecombe Whitefaced Dartmoor sheep were wonderful mothers producing good lambs and quality wool, which in the olden days brought much wealth to the district and the county.

The numbers of stock on offer at these fairs has fluctuated during the years and Widecombe Fair sold its last sheep in 1938. Tradition has to be maintained, however, and it is thanks to a determined group of people that Widecombe Fair was restarted after World War II, more as a show and sports event than a sale.

Tradition must be kept alive and there is saying that **Tradition and Folklore must be accepted as fact until disproved** and the people of Widecombe must do their best to ensure that this tradition continues for generations to come.

Widecombe Fair, its song of *Uncle Tom Cobley and All* and the story associated with it must be held fast in the folklore of this area and most importantly passed on to future generations to maintain. As with all legends and folklore, Widecombe Fair is a story with elements of truth.

Dartmoor ponies

THE SONG

The song *Widecombe Fair* can be traced long before 1850. The words and tune varied according to the part of the country, but always had the same theme of Tom Pearse and Tom Cobley. By 1890 when the Reverend Sabine Baring-Gould, one of the first collectors of English folk songs, published it in his *Songs of the West*, it had become known in its present form. At the rear of that book it states the following:

'Song 16 Widdecombe Fair. At present the best known and most popular of Devonshire songs, though the melody is without particular merit. The original 'Uncle Tom Cobley' lived in a house near Yeoford Junction, in the parish of Spreyton. His will was signed on January 20, 1787, and was proved on March 14, 1794. He was a genial old bachelor. Mr Samuel Peach, his oldest relation living, tells me, "My great-uncle, who succeeded him, with whom I lived for some years, died in 1843, over eighty years of age; he married, but left no children." We have obtained numerous variants of the air, one taken down from R. Bickle, Two Bridges, is an early form of the melody; but as that we give is familiar to most Devonshire men, we have retained it. The names in the chorus all belonged to residents at Sticklepath. Mr C. Sharp has taken down a variant as 'Midsummer Fair' in Somersetshire. The words so far as they went were the same, but each verse ended in a jingle instead of names.'

The tune of *Widecombe Fair* was at one time used as the regimental march by the 5th Devon (Haytor) Volunteers before they merged with the Devonshire Regiment. It is said that the Devon Regiment of Volunteers marched to the tune in 1899 during the Boer War. The Devonshire Regiment subsequently merged with the Dorsets to become the Devonshire and Dorset Regiment, and then later became The Devon and Dorset Light Infantry when they continued to use the song in their regimental march. In 2007 The Devon and Dorsets were disbanded, their colours laid up in Exeter Cathedral and they amalgamated with other regiments and became The Rifles.

Many eminent people have put pen to paper regarding the history of this famous song. Vian Smith in his *Portrait of Dartmoor* refers to the Reverend S. Baring-Gould writing down a version in 1891. This was accredited to a Mr W. F. Collier of Horrabridge.

Vian Smith also noted that another version had been published in 1880 by a Mr W. Davies of Kingsbridge, and the tune noted by Mr H. Fleetwood Sheppard.

According to local historian, Bob Mann, another earlier version was popular in the South Hams area. This version included variations in tune and words, with an additional member of the riding party known as Bob Paul. Bob Mann also refers to a copy of the song collected at Harberton in 1913. In this version, the party never reached the Fair, the unfortunate mare expiring en route. Further research reveals that in 1971 folklorist, Peter Kennedy, published an article in the *Dartington Hall News*. His study of the origin of *Widecombe Fair* found similar 'Fair' songs had long existed in Cornwall, Somerset, Hampshire, Oxfordshire and Bedfordshire. Included in the various casts were such notables as Uncle Tom Cobber, Uncle Tom Cockerell and Uncle Joe Maybe. Also revealed was the different number of participants involved in the journey.

Peter Kennedy's research also uncovered the 1913 rendition as sung by Hamlyn Parsons of Harberton. Apart from the inclusion of Bob Paul, all the others are the current party, ie Bill Brewer, etc. However there are considerable differences in the demise of the old grey mare.

Peter Kennedy and other established folk singers make a strong case for a much earlier origin. The first publication, he suggests, was 1880, by Mr W. Davies of Kingsbridge. This was known as the 'Harberton version'. To collaborate this theory we return to Vian Smith. Writing in the *South Devon Journal* in 1955 under his pseudonym, Rowley, he examined the mummers' plays popular in the eighteenth century. In one of these, a character called Tom Pearce represented the devil. In this story, a man dies and is consigned to Tom Pearce. Death arrives in the guise of a white horse. Kennedy's research records touring mummers' plays, in which groups of heavily disguised men travel the country. One of them wore a white sheet and a horse's head. Is this the origin of 'horse play'?

Probably the most popular version is the one associated with the Reverend Sabine Baring-Gould. He started collecting folk songs of the Westcountry in 1890, assisted by singers from various backgrounds. In most cases, the words had to be written in situ, there being no recognised lyrics. His research into Widecombe Fair covered the county from Kingsbridge to Horrabridge. His earliest field notes recorded our song title as *Tavistock Fair*. However, Baring Gould eventually appeared to accept the version performed by Harry Westaway of Belstone. Although Baring-Gould was convinced of the existence of a real live Tom Pearse and Tom Cobley, he appears to have neglected the existence of Bob Paul who was in the Harberton version.

Then there is the strange affair of the number of verses. The Westaway family of Belstone recall the Reverend Sabine Baring-Gould interviewing their father on local folk songs. The Westaway *Widecombe Fair* contained nine verses, one more than Baring-Gould's long established version. According to the Westaway family, this ninth verse made reference to the old grey mare only being shod on one foot. Why it was never included remains a mystery, although correspondence

№ 16 WIDDECOMBE FAIR

1

"Tom Pearce, Tom Pearce, lend me your grey mare,
All along, down along, out along, lee.
For I want for to go to Widdecombe Fair,
Wi' Bill Brewer, Jan Stewer, Peter Gurney, Peter Davy, Dan'l Whiddon,
Harry Hawk, old Uncle Tom Cobbley and all,"
CHORUS: Old Uncle Tom Cobbley and all.

2

"And when shall I see again my grey mare?"
All along, &c.
"By Friday soon, or Saturday noon,
Wi' Bill Brewer, Jan Stewer, &c.

3

Then Friday came, and Saturday noon,
All along, &c.
But Tom Pearce's old mare hath not trotted home,
Wi' Bill Brewer, &c.

4

So Tom Pearce he got up to the top o' the hill
All along, &c.
And he seed his old mare down a making her will
Wi' Bill Brewer, &c.

5

So Tom Pearce's old mare, her took sick and died.
All along, &c.
And Tom he sat down on a stone, and he cried
Wi' Bill Brewer, &c.

6

But this isn't the end o' this shocking affair,
All along, &c.
Nor, though they be dead, of the horrid career
Of Bill Brewer, &c.

7

When the wind whistles cold on the moor of a night
All along, &c.
Tom Pearce's old mare doth appear, gashly white,
Wi' Bill Brewer, &c.

8

And all the long night be heard skirling and groans,
All along, &c.
From Tom Pearce's old mare in her rattling bones,
And from Bill Brewer, Jan Stewer, Peter Gurney, Peter Davy, Dan'l Whiddon,
Harry Hawk, old Uncle Tom Cobbley and all.
CHORUS: Old Uncle Tom Cobbley and all.

This is the most well known of Devon's folk songs and, as far as is known, was first published about 1880. The above version of this popular air was written down by the Reverend Sabine Baring-Gould, one of the first collectors of English folk songs. It is generally thought that Tom Pearse came from Spreyton and his friends from Sticklepath, two villages on the northern side of Dartmoor.

Certainly the best-known and most popular of all Devonshire airs. An older form of the melody is given in the MS. The original 'Uncle Tom Cobley' lived in a house near Yeoford Junction in the parish of Spreyton. The names in the chorus were all residents of Sticklepath. Printed in Songs of the West with verse 5 omitted. Cecil Sharp noted version 'Midsummer Fair' in Somerset. Sometimes the words ended with a jingle instead of names.

Widdecombe Fair

Taken down from W. F. Collier, Woodtown, 1888

1. "Tom Pearce, Tom Pearce, lend me your grey mare,   All along down along.

out along, lee,   For I want for to go — to   Widdecombe Fair, Wi' Bill

Brewer, Jan Stewer, Peter Gurney, Peter Davy, Dan'l Whiddon, Harry Hawk, old

Uncle Tom Cobbley and all, ___   old   Uncle Tom Cobbley and all."___

2. 'And when shall I see again my grey mare?'
   All along, etc.
   'By Friday soon, or Saturday noon,
   Wi' Bill Brewer, etc.

3. Then Friday came, and Saturday noon,
   All along, etc.
   But Tom Pearce's old mare hath not trotted home
   Wi' Bill Brewer, etc.

4. So Tom Pearce he got up to the top o' the hill
   All along, etc.
   And he seed his old mare down a-making her will
   Wi' Bill Brewer, etc.

5. And how did he know it was his grey mare?
   All along, etc.
   'Cos one foot was shod and the other was bare.
   Wi' Bill Brewer, etc.

6. So Tom Pearce's old mare, her took sick and died.
   All along, etc.
   And Tom he sat down on a stone, and he cried
   Wi' Bill Brewer, etc.

7. And now that Tom Pearce's old grey mare is dead,
   All along, etc.
   They all agreed that her should be buried
   Wi' Bill Brewer, etc.

8. But this isn't the end o' this shocking affair,
   All along, etc.
   Nor, though they be dead, of the horrid career
   Of Bill Brewer, etc.

9. When the wind whistles cold on the moor of a night
   All along, etc.
   Tom Pearce's old mare doth appear, gashly white,
   Wi' Bill Brewer, etc.

10. And all the long night be heard skirling and groans,
    All along, etc.
    From Tom Pearce's old mare in her rattling bones,
    And from Bill Brewer, Jan Stewer, Peter Gurney,
    Peter Davy, Dan'l Whiddon,
    Harry Hawk, old Uncle Tom Cobbley and all.
    Chorus Old Uncle Tom Cobbley and all.

via the *Western Morning News* in 1948 confirmed there was plenty of knowledge of the ninth verse.

Another ninth verse, according to the *News Chronicle* of 12th September 1934, was discovered in the Dunn family Bible on the eve of the 1934 Widecombe Fair by Edward Dunn's sister. Edward Dunn had taken the role of Uncle Tom Cobley since 1928, and claimed that he was the great great grandson of the original Uncle Tom. This additional verse refers to the reimbursement to Tom Pearse for the dead grey mare.

TOM PEARSE'S OLD MARE TOOK SICK & DIED.

So they all came home from Widecombe Fair
All along, down along, out along lee.
They buried the other and bought Tom Pearse another
Did Bill Brewer, Jan Stewer, Peter Gurney,
Peter Davy, Dan'l Whiddon, Harry Hawk,
Old Uncle Tom Cobley and all, Old Uncle Tom Cobley and all.

Other well known Grey Mares are the Welsh 'Mari Lwyd' and Cornwall's colourful 'Obby Oss' at Padstow. Variations in the number and names of the riding party existed even within the boundaries of Dartmoor. The late Bob Cann MBE, inspiration of the Dartmoor Folk Festival, had his own version. This was passed on to him by his father, included one extra rider, and contained seven different names to those in popular use today. This version is also attributed to Bill Westaway who performed it at Belstone in 1950, and it is still performed today.

Continuous research into Uncle Tom's journey to Widecombe uncovers further folk songs associated with the village. Peter Kennedy unearthed *Jolly Companions of Widlicombe Fair* sung by Harry Cox of Catfield in 1953. The companions on this particular journey to the 'Widlicombe Fair' consisted of the local baker, local cobbler, local weaver, etc, but no mention of a grey mare. There is another version which uses the current tune but has a completely different crew. This journey appeared to start at Mary Tavy and a week in St Ives is the objective. Ron Rich takes the place of Tom Pearce, and his van replaced the old grey mare. Unfortunately the van met the same fate as the mare, expired in a cloud of steam on Sourton Hill.

From the coast of East Devon drifts up the same musical theme. This time the words pay tribute to a hard working group of cliff farmers. Assisted by donkeys instead of grey mares, they hauled seaweed from Branscombe, and spread this on their steep sided potato fields. Eventually their crops are gathered in and transported to Sidmouth market by horse and cart. In the rhyme, Uncle Tom Cobley converts to Uncle Frank Woodrow, also the entire crew have different names.

In 1995 the Wren Trust arranged a theatrical event at Sticklepath. This was called 'Tom Pearce's Legacy'. It included a mummers' play plus a hobby horse. Paul Wilson and Marilyn Tucker composed and presented *The Song of the Widows*. This referred to the demise of widows Brewer, Stewer, Gurney, Davey, Whiddon and Hawk. No one grieved for Uncle Tom Cobleigh. The Sticklepath event was commemorated by the laying of a mosaic depicting the old grey mare, which can still be seen at the rear of Finch's Foundry.

Pamela Colman Smith was a popular book illustrator, specialising in lithoprints. In 1899 she designed and illustrated a song book of *Widdicombe Fair*. The figures appear in period costume, lavishly clothed with faces full of character. There is a very interesting variation in the story which adds drama and sex where none previously existed. Once at the Fair, the riders disperse to a variety of entertainments. One of them engages in conversation with a gypsy girl, which finally develops into the couple galloping off across the moor on the old grey mare. This story line continues in colourful style until the final illustration. The finale gives us a very detailed view of a churchyard, probably Sticklepath, in which are a variety of gravestones and memorials. On these gravestones are inscribed the names of most of the riders of the old grey mare. There is a copy of this wonderfully illustrated book in the Westcountry Studies Library in Exeter.

Another version of the song appears in an equally colourful publication, sponsored by Whiteways and produced in 1937. It was based on an illustration by I. Richards from 1916. This was a dual purpose booklet, telling the usual story of the grey mare, but also extolling the joys of Whiteways Cider, at two shillings

Oh to be a cliff farmer!

They'd work on they cliff from morning till night
Al la-long, down a-long, out a-long lee
And never dig teddies till time was just right
With Jack Northcott, Cliffy Gosling, Bill Perryman, George Lee, Bill Ward,
Sammy Gill, Old Uncle Frank Woodrow and all -
Old Uncle Frank Woodrow and all.

Their donkeys full-loaded are down on the beach
All a-long, down a-long etc...
Now they're climbing up cliff-path till plats they do reach
With Jack Northcott etc...

What made them stick at it - to sweat and to toil?
All a-long, down a-long lee etc...
'T'was digging the seaweed that sweetened the soil
with Jack Northcott etc...

Now they're off to Sidmouth with horse and with cart
All a-long, down a-long etc...
With a load of new teddies and pride in their heart
With Jack Northcott etc...

They whistle and sing as they go on their way
All a-long, down a-long etc...
And thank the good Lord for this wonderful day
With Jack Northcott etc...

Then come the big night - cost a leg and an arm!
All a-long, down a-long etc...
Their rent was to pay up at that Berry Farm
With Jack Northcott etc...

Farmer White he would greet them - he'd not much to say
All a-long, down a-long etc...
They'd rented the plats, and now they must pay

Well, now they've all gone to their home in the sky
All a-long, down a-long etc...
If they could plant teddies I bet they would try
With Jack Northcott etc...

And if you should walk out on the cliffs of a night
All a-long, down a-long etc...
You'll see all they donkeys appear ghastly white

An East Devon version of the famous Song

a gallon. A total of eight illustrations tell the story. These illustrations are held in copyright by John Harrap and Son, Publishers, Holborn, London.

These pictures were used to popularise Whiteways Cider

Sticklepath Graveyard as depicted by Pamela Coleman Smith, 1899

In 1938, Oxford University Press published a range of sheet music, promoting popular pieces of chamber music for students. These musical arrangements were produced by eminent musicians of the day, such as the distinguished conductor, John Barbirolli. The musical score for *Widecombe Fair* was produced by Arthur Trew, and sold for one shilling. It was arranged for a string orchestra which consisted of two violins, a viola, cello and bass, with an option for piano accompaniment. They were advertised as suitable for teaching and for concert performance. The Widecombe and District Local History Group has a copy of this musical score in their archives.

The popularity of the tale of the old grey mare is very evident by the number of books published on the subject. George Adamson produced one such book in 1966. Baring-Gould receives credit for the melody. Adamson's art work produced characters that could have come straight out of *Punch* magazine.

Another book which had great similarity to Pamela Colman Smith's work was produced by Patricia Lee Gauch in 1978. Titled *On to Widecombe Fair* it was beautifully illustrated by Trina Schart Hyman. They actually stayed in Widecombe whilst producing the book, an acknowledgement to 'Old Walls Farm' precedes the story. The illustrations show many recognisable views of the district, and many local place names are used.

Some interesting alternative story lines also appear in this version.The discussion by the infamous group takes place at The Duke's Head, an inn somewhere near Spreyton. The nearest inn that has a similar name is the Duke of York at Iddesleigh. After a failed journey attempt by donkey and cart, they manage to acquire a grey mare. The illustrations depicted the trip to Widecombe with six men walking and one in the saddle. The text indicates that each took a turn in the saddle with Uncle Tom Cobley riding the horse into the Fairground. The group then settled down to a very long period of drinking and merrymaking. Assuming the Fair was held on its usual Tuesday date, by late Saturday none of them could manage to walk back to Spreyton. So the return journey started out with seven drunkards clinging, in a scrumpy induced stupor, to a sagging grey mare. The lamentable end occurred near Beetor Cross. The whole book is a very colourful interpretation and contains much to interest local readers.

Over the years many postcards have been produced showing Tom Cobley with the grey mare and quoting the song. One of the earliest hand drawn postcards of Widecombe Fair was published in around 1906 by T. Carin and Son of Bovey Tracey.

A thirteen card series illustrating the whole episode was produced by Ashburton photographer, E. S. Scott. He used local people to re-enact every scene. These subsequently became collectors' items. Eventually 'the entrepreneur of all Uncle Tom Cobleys', Edward Dunn, recognised their potential and assumed his marketing role.

Messrs Chapman & Son and Valentines, nationally renowned postcard manufacturers, also produced cards promoting 'Widdicum Vare' in about 1920.

Ruth of Ashburton, Valentines, Raphael Tuck and Sons, Bamforth and Colourmaster all produced Widecombe Fair cards, not forgetting the booklet of cards by P. R. Middleweek entitled *A Devonshire Man's Original Impression of Widecombe Fair* designed and printed by W. Chudley and Son.

Postcards can be found in junk shops, on market stalls, book and postcard fairs and on ebay. They show the changes in transport, fashion and the surrounding landscape. No doubt publications on Widecombe Fair will continue to appear and theorists will continue their quest for its origin.

To end these observations on the story and music of *Widecombe Fair*, we

Postcards produced by Chapman & Son, Dawlish

24

Postcards produced by Chapman & Son, Dawlish

have noted international interest.

In 2002, Boris and Myrna Klapwald from New York visited the Sticklepath/ Spreyton area. Their quest was the origin of the Widecombe Fair story. A recent conversation with Boris has revealed their reason for such a quest. They have developed a deep interest in the origins of American folk music. They visited England with a large number of folk music queries, seeking musical roots and subsequent folk tales. Widecombe Fair was just one of several Westcountry based research items. Due to a health problem, the trip was curtailed, never completed. However, Boris subsequently stated that the tune to *Widecombe Fair* exists in many guises in the USA. His research has found the tune in use with a variety of different words in several States. One particular line of research had taken them from tobacco plantations, across the Atlantic to Bristol, home of cigarette giants, W. D. & H. O. Wills. Bristol's association with slavery is already well documented.

There are many questions unanswered – is the song based on fact, legend or myth? The ghost of the old grey mare continues to lead us on a never ending merry dance.

- Without doubt, research has indicated that the storyline is ageless. Over the years the names of the cast have varied, however the existence of an 'Old Uncle' appears in most versions.

- The song has been sung in village halls and concert parties with local names being substituted for the traditionally accepted version.

- The location also has many variations, but events generally centre on a Fair.

- The one solitary item that exists in the majority of the versions is that most essential GREY MARE.

- How many people went to Widecombe Fair? The answer is often given as seven but, in fact, it was eight as 'I' went with the other seven characters. Who was 'I'? Could it have been Uncle Tom's nephew, whose name appears on the gravestone in Spreyton Churchyard?

- Taking it one step further, who or what was 'All'? We know that one of Uncle Tom's dogs was called 'Spot' and he was buried near Colebrook. Could he have had another one called 'All'?

Thomas Cobley's headstone in Spreyton Churchyard

Transcription of Thomas Cobley's headstone

THE CAST

In *The Guardian* of 26th February 1993, the question was posed:

'Did Bill Brewer, Jan Stewer, Peter Gurney, Peter Davey, Dan'l Whiddon, Harry Hawk, to say nothing of Thomas Cobbleigh, actually exist?' The answer, given by Dr Geoffrey Irlam of South Zeal, was: "YES, and so did Tom Pearse, from whom they borrowed the unfortunate grey mare in the song.

"The Pearse family moved to Sticklepath on the edge of Dartmoor in the early years of the 19th century. They were woolstaplers – Tom's house, Staplers, is still in the village – and in 1810 they built a water-powered serge mill on the banks of the River Taw. The mill's bright red cloth was particularly highly thought of. Large quantities were exported to India for the uniforms of the bodyguard of the Nizam of Hyderabad.

"Tom Pearse was a staunch Methodist and it is perhaps surprising that he lent the transport for what was surely a drinking spree at the fair at Widecombe, some twelve miles over the Moor. The names mentioned in the song, incidentally, are all local. Tom Cobbleigh came from Buxford, near Spreyton, about three miles from Sticklepath. There's a pub there which bears his name."

Uncle Tom Cobley's Home
Buxford. Devon

It is worth mentioning that strict Methodists would not have drunk alcohol. Also that the visit to the Fair was not a 'drinking spree' but a serious day's business.

The wool of the Dartmoor sheep was ideal for producing a good quality serge cloth and it was also used for carpets.

The editor of the *Devonian Year Book 1942*, Francis Perry, published his own research on Thomas Cobley of Spreyton. He quoted a search of Crediton Parish Church records by Preb. W. M. Smith-Dorrien. This research managed to associate Thos. Cobley with other parishioners of Crediton bearing the names of Stewer, Davy and Hawkes.

Tom Pearse makes a good starting point as a well-established resident of

Sticklepath. In 1818 his father, John Pearse, moved from Horrabridge (that name again) to open a serge mill at Skaigh Hill. This was on the parish borders of Sticklepath and Belstone. Tom was born in 1793, an important date! If the proposed excursion to Widecombe had departed from Spreyton in 1802, he was only nine years old. So, with the first name there is a query. In 1830 he became a prime mover in a merger between the Quakers of Sticklepath and the growing Methodist movement. At that time, the serge mill was in full production and products were transported to Plymouth and Exeter by horse-drawn wagons. Father, John Pearse, was an accomplished horseman and must have owned a large stable. Records show that

Tom Pearse of Sticklepath

he regularly rode a return day trip from Sticklepath to Exeter, a distance of forty miles.

A recent meeting with a member of the Pearse family, Carrel Jevons, has not revealed any direct connection with Tom Cobley. However there is a possible connection between the Pearse family and Baring Gould. John Pearse, the Hatherleigh poet, was a nephew of Tom Pearse. John M. Martin, writing in *Devon & Cornwall Notes and Queries 1912* mentioned a meeting in 1850 with John Pearse at the Dartmoor Inn, mid way between Tavistock and Okehampton. The Inn was full of cattle dealers and produce dealers after a busy day at Tavistock market. The next day they would be in business in Okehampton. Folksinging and poetry reading made up the entertainment. These social gatherings were an old established tradition, noted also by William Crossing. An Inn with such a tradition for folk music would have been a great incentive for Baring-Gould in his quest for folk music in the making.

John Martin also reported that "It is worth noting that, in his quest for songs from the moor, Baring-Gould had some success in Widecombe. Among local contributors were Mary Roberts of Scobbetor, Roger Hannaford of South Widdecombe, Richard Cleve of the Forest Inn, Mary Satcherly of Huccaby, and Jonas Coker of Postbridge."

Baring-Gould's book, *Songs and Ballads of the West*, contains 110 collected folk songs, and *Widecombe Fair* is undoubtedly one of the oldest survivors. Whoever the originators of *Widecombe Fair* were, they could not have selected a more illustrious character than Uncle Tom Cobley.

However, before delving into the background of Uncle Tom, if the connection with Widecombe Fair is to be verified, dates of subsequent events need careful scrutiny as there were a

Tom Pearse's Headstone in the Quaker Burial Ground at Sticklepath

Portrait of Tom Cobley with his dog, Spot, in Spreyton Tavern

number of Tom Cobleys. Was it a family tradition to go to Widecombe Fair?

For a short period of history, the name – Thomas Cobley – was very popular in the Spreyton area. Research has shown that there were up to six Tom Cobleys in the period 1698-1844. The one who fits best was born 1762, died 1844 and lived in Butsford. This would also fit with information on the Tavern Sign.

To add confusion to conclusion, various writers over the years have suggested that the other members of the trip were established local men. Families bearing all the surnames in the song can be traced in various parishes in the mid-Devon area.

POSSIBLE ROUTES TO THE FAIR

If the journey to Widecombe Fair was undertaken with a horse and cart/wain/wagon, the team would have stayed on the roads rather than open moor, a possible route being to Chagford, via Whiddon Down, then to Beetor Cross and along Long Lane to Heatree Cross and on to Widecombe.

Vian Smith, in his book *A Portrait of Dartmoor*, suggested a route to Widecombe, via Cawsand, Challacombe and Hamel Down. The distance was recorded in excess of fourteen miles, leaving at 5.00am and arriving at 11.00am. Apparently they arrived in time for the sheep sales, which were followed by 'drinking, dumb shows and dancing'.

On 10th September 1996, Sarah Nosworthy and Sarah Mortimore re-enacted the ride on horseback from Spreyton to Widecombe Fair. This is the route they used, devised by Sarah Nosworthy.

"We left from outside Spreyton Church and followed the road to Brandis Cross. On the way we passed a field of sunflowers on the left near Fuidge Manor. At Brandis Cross we turned left onto the B3219, Whiddon Down – North Tawton road. Along this road we had to cross the bridge over the A30 on our way to Whiddon Down, where we crossed the A382 (old A30) and rode up a side road before taking a right into Chapel Road. At the top we crossed the A382 again (now Moretonhampstead – Whiddon Down road). Once across we rode along this road to take first left at Tor View. The road we turned into was very long and

Outside Spreyton Church.

boring until we found a field of pigs on the right. At the crossroads we went straight across and rode past a house called 'Mount Flaggon'. We turned right at the T junction and rode down the steep hill past Washford Barn, crossing the River Teign at the bottom and onto another crossroads by the Mid Devon Hunt Kennels.

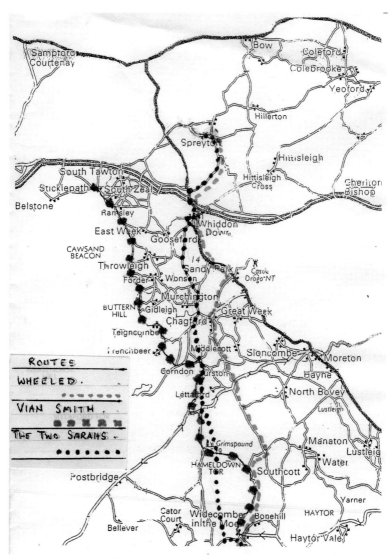

Plan showing possible routes to the Fair

"We then started a steady climb out of Chagford towards Waye Barton going straight over the staggered crossroads. We went past Buda (where the Thoroughbred stallion Battlement stood at stud for several years) and along beneath Meldon Hill and left at the T junction. At the next junction (below Downes) we turned right and then straight on to Yellands Cross where we turned right again. This road took us down to Jurston Bridge and then past Jurston. After this we had our first and only cattle grid, before heading onto the open moor and beginning the steep descent into Green Coombe, to cross the stream and bog at the bottom, before climbing towards the B.3212 and riding up over Shapley Common.

"This part of the ride had the most fantastic views and we could see for miles. After riding past Shapley Tor, we continued until we met the wall that runs above Kingsbarrow and Hookner. At the top we crossed the broken down wall that runs up from the Challacombe road near Headland Warren. We then rode along the well worn track towards King Tor. There was a branch right which took us across to the Grimspound track and we travelled over the heather to meet the track that ran across the top of Hameldown from the RAF stone to Hameldown Beacon.

"Riding along the top of Hameldown, we passed several wooden posts. These were erected during the World War II to stop any German planes landing. Whilst riding along the top we passed Broad, Single and Two Barrows before riding along the Blackaton wall to Hameldown Beacon. From then it was downhill all the way, passing the top wall of Kingshead Farm and heading down the track towards Two Crosses at the top of Southcombe. We then travelled across the moor before joining the road to go down Southcombe Hill and arrived in the Fair Field at the bottom of the hill.

"The ride was completed in one hour and seventeen minutes - a total of approximately seventeen miles". This distance is similar to Vian Smith's calculation.

Arriving at Widecombe Fair.

33

WIDECOMBE FAIR SITES

The Fair has been held on several different sites in and around the village, the original being on the Village Green. This led to the expression that, in Widecombe, 'sheep were sold by the yard' because the sheep were penned against the Churchyard wall.

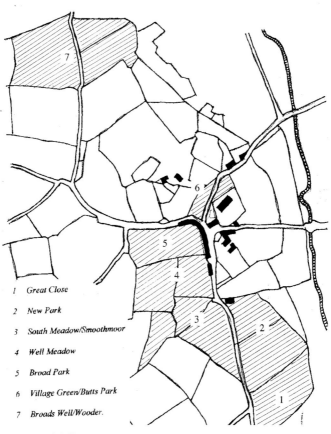

1   Great Close

2   New Park

3   South Meadow/Smoothmoor

4   Well Meadow

5   Broad Park

6   Village Green/Butts Park

7   Broads Well/Wooder.

Map of different Fair Sites

In the years 1922 to 1926, the Fair was held in South Meadow (now known as Smooth Moor). It was let to the Fair Committee by Mr John Hannafordof Southcombe. In 1926 a deposit of £2 was demanded which would be refunded provided all sports equipment was removed within a week of the event. This field is now the site of Widecombe County Primary School.

In 1927 it was held in Well Meadow and the adjoining field by kind permission of

Mr John Hannaford. These fields are closer to the Village Well (often referred to as the Saxon Well) which was, for many years, the main source of water for the village. Some people still exercise their right to draw water from this Well.

1928 saw the Fair returned to South Meadow. No reason has been found for the move away in 1927. In 1929 and 1930, the Fair was held in Broad Park behind the Old Inn by kind permission of the Landlord, Mr Broughton.

In 1931 and 1932, the Fair was again held behind the Old Inn with parking in Goodish Meadow, the sheep in Well Meadow and pony classes and sports in Broad Park.

Between 1933 and 1938 the Fair took place in New Park courtesy of Mr Jasper French, although, in 1933, it was stated that 'the ground must be cleared up afterwards' and a deposit of £5 was charged, refundable if the site was left tidy. In 1938, however, Jasper French stated he 'would require £15 compensation for the use of his fields, explaining that the fields comprised ten acres of his best land'. It was agreed he should have this amount. However, on some occasions, the sheep were still penned by the Churchyard wall.

There was no Fair held in the years 1939-1944 due to World War II, but in 1945 a modified Fair on the Village Green was arranged at short notice following the end of the War.

1946 found the Fair being held in Great Close – now the site of the main car park. In 1947 and 1948 the Fair moved to a site north of the village on fields belonging to Wooder Farm.

In 1949 the Fair was held once again on New Park, sometimes referred to on the programmes as 'The Old Field', and it has remained on this site to date, with Great Close and Church Meadow being used as car parks. With the constant growth in traffic, various additional fields have been used for car parks. The Committee has now a right of easement in perpetuity on fields on Southcombe Lane to further secure the car parking arrangements for future years.

HIGHLIGHTS OF YESTERYEAR

1802 As previously mentioned, on the exterior wall of the Uncle Tom Cobley Tavern at Spreyton, the Inn sign states: 'The Tom Cobley Tavern. Licensed 1589. From this Village of Spreyton on a day in September 1802, the following left for Widdecombe Fair. Bill Brewer, Jan Stewer, Peter Gurney, Peter Davey, Dan'l Widden, Harry Hawke and Uncle Tom Cobley andAll'.

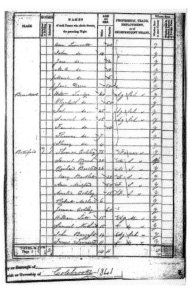

1841. *This is the year of the first National Census and shows the Cobley family living at Colebrook, near Spreyton.*

Name	Age	Occupation	Relationship ?
Thomas Cobley	70	Farmer	*Batchelor*
Sammual Roach	20	MS	*Nephew*
Richard Bartlett	26	MS	*Nephew*
Mary Bartlett	30	FS	*Niece*
Ann Mitford	50	FS	*NK*
Amelia Cobley	15	FS	*Niece*
Robert Medland	16	MS	*Servant*
Joanna Cobley	60	FS	*Sister*
William Lott	15	MS	*Hired Help*
Sammual Northcott	15	MS	"
John Burgess	14	Agricultural Lab	*NK*
James Townsend	11	"	*NK*
James Longman	12	"	*Nk*

Interpretation of 1841 Census

36

1850 A report in 1850 is one of the earliest written records of Widecombe Fair that has been found. In that year, the Fair took place on Tuesday, 29th October on the Village Green and it was reported that there was a large attendance of yeoman and gentlemen of the district. This would appear to have been a Fair and a Sale of Sheep, Cattle and Ponies. 736 sheep were penned. 75 store and fatted beasts were sold, plus 4 bulls. A South Devon cow reared by the Reverend J. H. Mason sold for £15.10s.0d. About 50 ponies were also driven in. The Vicar, who was well known for his hospitality held a large dinner party (see introduction) and celebrated the Fair in 'Fine Old English Style'.

1876 Widecombe School records show that the school was closed in the afternoon on account of the Fair being held. Very few children were in school during the morning or on the Wednesday!

1879 There were no children at school on Fair Day and a holiday was given in consequence. This extra holiday continued to be given over the following years.

1882 *The Western Morning News* reported that 'The fair at Widecombe-in-the-Moor took place on Tuesday. This annual gathering of moorland farmers was held on the Village Green and the ancient archery butts. There was a full average attendance of buyers and sellers and, notwithstanding the recent auction sales in the neighbourhood of the stocks of outgoing tenants, a brisk business was done, especially in sheep. On the evening of the fair, an entertainment of a kind unusual in this quiet village was got up for the benefit of the funds of the Ashburton and Buckfastleigh Cottage Hospital. The use of the large schoolroom in the upper story of the ancient Church-house being readily granted by the School Board, a choice selection of music, songs and readings was given by ladies and gentlemen, residents and visitors of the neighbourhood'.

1907 In 1907 it is recorded that a large show of cattle and moorland sheep was held.

1913 A newspaper article appeared entitled 'Uncle Tom Cobley and All at Widecombe Races', the opening paragraph of which stated 'I have seen the Derby at Epsom. I have been to Ascot and one or two of the lesser known race meetings of this country, but I say without the least hesitation that none of them is exactly like the Widecombe event. Although the 'classics' may differ from each other in certain details – one may be more fashionable than another – yet as far as their leading features are concerned they are alike. That is just where Widecombe differs. There aren't any leading features, unless it is the features of the natives, which are so much alike – whiskers for age – that it is difficult to tell sometimes whether the individual you are talking to is really himself or the man behind him.'

Later in the article the author tells his readers that 'Widecombe is hidebound by no conventionalities. Nobody would feel called upon to comment if a jockey turned out in pyjamas or a garment of his wife's, or his Sunday-best tweed suit complete with bowler hat and lavender tie. All this lends a delightful novelty to the races. The medley of types, the open moor, the proud tors, the near sky, and through all the rich round Devon dialect and the great, rare Devon laugh 'do's anybody gude'.

51ST YEAR. NO. 36. 1913 [Registered at the General Post Office as a Newspaper]. NEW
Sat 13th September Page 1

Some of the Types Sketched by Mr. Charles Lane Vicary

UNCLE TOM COBLEY AND ALL

AT WIDECOMBE RACES.

I have seen the Derby at Epsom. I have been to Ascot and one or two of the lesser known race meetings of this country, but I say, without the least hesitation that none of them is exactly like the Widecombe event.

Although the "classics" may differ from each other in certain details—one may be more fashionable than another—yet as far as their leading features are concerned they are alike.

That is just where Widecombe differs. There aren't any leading features, unless it is the features of the natives, which are so much alike—whiskers for age—that it is difficult to tell sometimes whether the individual you are talking to is really himself or the man behind him.

The small farmer who just "strolls up around to see the sport." He can gaze for a long time in the same direction but has a remarkable gift for "taking it all in."

At the ordinary race-meetings such as Newmarket and Doncaster, or even Newton and Totnes, all the riders wear more or less uniform suits. Different colours, of course, but all modelled on the same plan, with caps of recognised shape, and riding-breeches and spurs.

Widecombe is hide bound by no such conventionalities. Nobody would feel called upon to comment if a jockey turned out in pyjamas, or a garment of his wife's, or his Sunday-best tweed suit complete with bowler hat and lavender tie. All this lends a delightful novelty to the races. You get

right away from the monotonous langua of the orthodox meeting. You miss together the everlasting "cerise" man sash," "blue gold hoops hedge, tap and so on. At Widecombe you back th rider with the corduroy trousers and t pink and string braces, or the one in the sh sleeves, red belt and hat new seat.

The smart young man who buys a screw of paper for five shillings into which a man has put a sovereign and a shilling. He has just discovered that the paper contained two halfpennies, and he is wondering how it is done.

The medley of types, the open moor, the proud tors, the near sky, and through all the rich, round Devon dialect and the great rare Devon laugh "do's anybody gude."

Last Saturday was the fourth annual meeting at Widecombe. The races are due to the good sport of the Vicary family.

What it means to them in expense and labour is, of course, their own affair. But as far as the public is concerned Widecombe Races make one of the quaintest and most enjoyable days on the moors one can imagine. There is no entrance fee, and no grand stand. You stand where you like. If you have a vehicle nobody orders you to put it here or there. You can just pitch it anywhere you like from Haytor Rock to Bowerman's Nose. I can't imagine anybody saying unkind things to you even if you stuck it across the course. The committee would probably immediately turn the next race into

From the Mid Devon Advertiser 1913

The visitor from the town who makes a day of it. He makes jokes incessantly and is usually the only one who laughs at them.

Of course, there is just a little danger in this sometimes. On one occasion I wanted to put a shilling on the "grey suit, brown boots, soft hat and whiskers." He was leading by several lengths and I thought he stood a good chance of winning. When I pointed him out to the bookmaker I learnt that I was trying to back the clerk of the course. I also learnt several other things from the bystanders which would not look well here.

There being a clerk of the course must not be taken to imply that there is any course. What I mean is, I wouldn't like anybody to stay away from the Widecombe meeting for fear of being hustled or pushed about as you are at some places. Certainly, it does happen that every now and then somebody on a horse dashes round like a fire engine, and says "Clear the course," but I am sure he would fall off his mount in surprise if you were to obey. As long as the crowd keeps clear of his elbows on both sides there will be plenty of room for the "field."

Cider is a very important factor in the day's proceedings especially for those who walk ten miles or so.

Fancy a race meeting in the heart of "Dartymoor." If you haven't seen it, you ought. You needn't be nervous. Whoever you are you will meet somebody there like you. Don't think you will look obvious if you go out in a car; you will find several there better than your own. On the other hand, don't mind in the least going in a wheelbarrow. Also your sandwiches and your drinks. If you have brought something in a black quart bottle don't feel called upon to get behind a great stone to quench your thirst. Stand in the middle of the course and have a good pull at it. The starter won't in the least mind waiting till you have finished. In fact I wouldn't be at the course. The committee would probably immediately turn the next race into a steeplechase. And while a race is on, in the interval between the time when the horses

The farmer who comes "mounted, booted, and spurred." He is very keen; rides about all day, shouts to the people to "clear the course," and usually manages to get in everybody's way himself.

disappear down one tor till they come up the next, you can have a perfectly delightful stroll across the moor and pick heather.

I have been to a Royal Derby and I have been to Ascot and to many other meetings. I would not trouble to stretch myself out straight to go to either of them again. But I hope I shall have the chance of seeing Widecombe Races next year. They were real sport. Wouldn't Uncle Tom Cobbley have enjoyed them, and Bill Brewer, Jan Stewer, Peter Gurney, Peter Davey, Dan'l Whiddon and 'Arry Awk. They were all there if we could only have seen them.

A.J.C.

From the Mid Devon Advertiser 1913

Some of the Types Sketched by Mr. Charles Lane Vicary

AT WIDECOMBE RACES.

The farmer who comes " mounted, booted, and spurred.". He is very keen ; rides about all day, shouts to the people to " clear the course," and usually manages to get in everybody's , way himself.

The smart young man who buys a screw of paper for five shillings into which a man has put a sovereign and a shilling. He has just discovered that the paper contained two halfpennies, and he is wondering how it is done.

The small farmer who just " strolls up" around to see the sport,". He can gaze for a long time in the same direction but has a remarkable gift for " taking it all in."

The visitor from the town who makes a day of it. He makes jokes incessantly and is usually the only one who laughs at them.

Cider is a very important factor in the day's proceedings especially for those who walk ten miles or so.

From the Mid Devon Advertiser 1913

40

1914 – 1918 Widecombe Fair seems to have continued as a cattle, sheep, pony and horse Fair, right through World War I.

1920 The late Hermon French recalled his father taking sheep to Widecombe Fair in the early 1920s, where they were penned against the Churchyard wall - the grass on the opposite side of the road to what is now known as the Green.

Uncle Tom Cobley an' All. The old ballad *Widdecombe Fair,* provided the inspiration for this sign for Widdecombe -in-the Moor, Devon. The designer Mr Joseph M. Doran was awarded a prize of £50 in the *Daily Mail* Village Sign Competition.

WIDDICOMBE FAIR

FAMOUS SONG SUNG AT VILLAGE SIGN UNVEILING

Awarded a special prize of £50 in the *Daily Mail's* Village Signs Competition in 1920, the Village Sign at Widdicombe, Devonshire, designed by Mr. J.M. Doran, 152, Finborough-road, Earl's Court, S.W., was unveiled on Saturday by Councillor Charles Stooke, chairman of the Newton Abbot Rural Council.

A feature of the ceremony was the singing of the Devonshire "anthem" "Widdicombe Fair". Two inhabitants of the village - Mr. C. Churchward and Mr. F. Gough - sang through the many verses of the old-world song without a hitch and the Visitors had some trouble in understanding the string of names sung in the broad dialect - Bill Brewer, Jan Stewer, Peter Gurney, Dan'l Widdon, 'Arry 'Awke, old Uncle Tom Cobley, and others, all of whom are pictured on the sign riding on Tam Pearse's old mare that bore its burden patiently - and then died from exhaustion. It is showing no sign of its inpending death in the picture - it had apparently just begun its journey.

The sign is an imposing one and is made from rough-hewn granite from a tor close by. At the top of the column are the name of the village in gold letters and the picture of the mare and her burden in painted tiles.

Mr. Stooke said it was a happy thought of the Duke of York, at the Royal Academy banquet in 1920 to suggest the revival of village signs, and, the *Daily Mail* had shown its usual enterprise in giving effect to the suggestion. Obviously, it was an advantage to motorists to know what village they were passing through. This was the first village sign erected in Devonshire.

Transcribed from the Daily Mail of the 17th July 1922

A report of the Daily Mail Village Sign Competition

Unveiling of the Widecombe Village Sign, 1922

Plaque on the Village Sign

The Prize Winning Sign

42

1921 The children's sports programme was prepared by Mrs Bates, headmistress of Widecombe School. Tea was provided in the schoolroom and subsequently there was dancing on the Village Green to the strains of the Bovey Band.

1922 The number of stock being presented for sale had been reduced considerably by this year. It is recorded that Widecombe Fair took place on Tuesday 12th September 1922 (this is the first reference found of the Fair being held on the second Tuesday in September). Only 1 sheep and 2 rams were presented for sale and none of them sold. This, it was considered, was due to the other regular markets being held in towns around the Moor like Newton Abbot, which were more attractive and great social events. However, in the afternoon, the Ashburton Band led the way to the sports field where a full programme was watched by a large crowd despite the very wet weather. According to the *Western Morning News*, the Reverend McCrea suggested 'that the open events should be run off so that the competitors from a distance should not be disappointed.' A reporter from *The Devon & Exeter Gazette* published this account on 15th September 1922 – 'We followed the band and, arriving at the entrance gate, paid our entrance money. I asked a man with a huge rosette in his buttonhole (he 'was on the Committee') if we could bring the car into the field, as the roadway was so narrow, besides our chauffer wanted to see the sports and his contribution thereto would lessen their financial troubles. "Thee must ask that there gennelman over there" he said, pointing him out. "No" said the gennelman "if I allows 'ee inside we may 'ave vorty thousand more wanting to cum in". We counted the cars. There were three, the one that brought the band from Ashburton, ours and one other. The sports programme was a very good and full one, so were the clouds with 'Dartmoor dew', for it was pelting with rain and we decided to leave Widecombe to its Fair and sports'. There was a concert and dance in the evening which was a great success.

1923 Due to the lack of sheep in the 1922 Fair, the Fairs in 1923 to 1926 had less of an agricultural content. More activities were introduced making the day more of a sports day, with children's races and pony classes. A Band was hired to play during the afternoon. After the sports the children marched with the Band to the North Hall Café (now the site of the playing field) for tea, provided at the cost of one shilling a head. The Vicar, the Reverend E. C. Wood, was 'in clerical dress and straw boater, strutting around the Fair'.

1924 Bovey Tracey Silver Band came to the Fair, men and boys, in very smart uniforms but their repertoire was limited as they played hymns for the musical posts on horseback! Fred Miners was the long jump champion. Permission to put a door in the back of the garage into South Meadow to sell refreshments was refused.

WIDECOMBE FAIR.

Sports Programme

9th SEPTEMBER, 1924.

The Sports begin at 2.15 with Races for Children.

		1st s. d.	2nd s. d.	3rd s. d.
1.	Quarter-Mile Race, under 17	7 0	5 0	2 6
2.	One Mile, Open	20 0	10 0	5 0
3.	Egg & Spoon Race, (Women)	6 0	4 0	2 0
4.	High Jump, Open	12 6	7 6	2 6
5.	100 Yards Race, (over 40)	7 0	5 0	2 6
6.	Half-Mile Race, Open	12 6	6 0	3 0
7.	220 yds. School Championship	5 0	3 0	1 6
8	Derby Boot Race	15 0	10 0	5 0
	INTERVAL.			
9.	Half-Mile Race	10 0	7 6	5 0
10.	Musical Chairs on Cycles	10 0	5 0	2 6
11.	Quarter-Mile Race, Open	10 0	5 0	2 6
12.	Band Race	5 0	3 0	1 6
13.	Potato Race on Horseback	15 0	10 0	5 0
14.	100 Yards Race	5 0	3 6	2 0
15.	Relay Race (teams of 4 from any one Parish)	10 0	4 0	
16.	Tug of War (teams of 8 from any one Parish)	45 0		

For Open Events, Entrance Fee 1/- to be paid to
Mr. Perkins or Mr Satterley, who will also take
Entries for all Races.
A Bell will be rung Two Minutes before each
Race starts.

J. F. BARKER, Caxton Printing Works, Ashburton.

Sports Programme 1924

1925 It was proposed that Miss Willcocks of North Hall Café and Mr Hall of the Moorland Café (now the Green Restaurant) should be approached as to terms for letting their rooms for a concert and dance on Sports Night. Also in 1925 it was decided to open a bank account and pay all debts by cheque. A pig should be obtained for Bowling for the Pig at a cost not to exceed £1.1s.0d. The 'Bye-Laws with respect to the Village Green' dated 1925, stated in Clause 4, that 'Nothing in these bye-laws shall in any respect prejudice or injuriously affect the use of the green for the purposes of the Annual Fair.'
1926 Discussion had taken place as to whether the sports should be held on the 21st August but it was agreed at a meeting held on 15th May to keep to the

WIDECOMBE - IN - THE - MOOR

TUG OF WAR TEAM, 1926

A. HORTON   H. NOSWORTHY   W. SATTERLEY   W. OLDRIEVE
T. NOSWORTHY   F. GOUGH   S. MINERS   S. NORRISH   W. MINERS

second Tuesday in September. It was decided to have pony classes and two classes for pens of Dartmoor Ewes (Whitefaced and Greyfaced). The prizes were £1, 10 shillings and 5 shillings. A Tug O' War competition took place.

1927 In April of 1927 it was agreed that the Fair should become more agricultural in its format and a determined effort was made to bring the Fair to its importance of ancient days. A group of three, Colonel Hankey, Canon E. F. Hall and Mr W. Kitson worked to revive the agricultural classes. This led to the Fair on Tuesday 13th September 1927 being extremely well supported by moorland farmers when between 600-700 sheep were penned on the Village Green and a great number of ponies and agricultural horses were offered for sale. A number of cups were presented and entry forms were received from all parts of the Westcountry.

Many charabancs brought visitors from Exeter, Torquay and Plymouth.

Mr W. J. Mann was appointed secretary for the agricultural side of the Fair.

For the first time for many years an auction sale of Dartmoor sheep was conducted.

1928 The Fair was favoured with ideal weather. There was a show and sale of 500 sheep. Ponies were exhibited and a silver cup was presented by Colonel Hankey for the Best Dartmoor Brood Mare shown at Widecombe Fair. The Cup was won by various people between 1929 and 1933, and then won outright by Mr. Gordon Daw of Natsworthy after he won it three years in succession in 1934, 1935 and 1936. It is still in the family's possession.

For the first time, an Uncle Tom Cobley impersonator was present on the field. Edward Dunn was the first known person to dress up and take the part of Uncle Tom Cobley on his Grey Mare. At the 1928 Fair a film was made based on the book *Widecombe Fair* written by Eden Phillpotts, first published in 1913. The film was shown in the London Hippodrome in 1929. 'Quote: Of the Dartmoor novels none was more popular in its day than *Widecombe Fair*. From its pages came a wildly successful play, *The Farmer's Wife*, and two films'.

1929 The revival of the Fair was justified by the large numbers attending. Two young ladies (Sylvia's Needham's sister being one of them) were so excited by their visit to the Fair that, when Mr Edward Dunn (Uncle Tom Cobley) went into the bar to get some refreshment, they 'hijacked' the Old Grey Mare and rode her around the village much to the consternation of Uncle Tom. Sylvia Needham also recalled that, once again, the band played hymns for the gymkhana event, Musical Poles. In 1929 Mr. Edward Dunn, farmer of Bonehill, was invited to join the Committee. However, there was great amusement on the day when Uncle Tom Cobley tumbled off the Old Grey Mare. One of the unusual events was a Tug O' War on horseback. It is recorded that the Leusdon

Edward Dunn, the first Uncle Tom Impersonator

team won with Widecombe in second place. However the following year the event was superseded by an obstacle race. Due to the number of show exhibits on the

Village Green, a further field had to be requisitioned to accommodate them all. However, the 1929 Fair only just covered expenses, at £120.

WIDECOMBE FAIR, C. 1930. Held on the second Tuesday in September, it was for centuries a market for large numbers of sheep, cattle and Dartmoor ponies. The fair still flourishes today, although it is now less agricultural in character.

1930 It was decided to appoint two secretaries to help with the organisation of the Fair. Mr. Kitson to cover the agricultural section and Canon E. F. Hall to cover the sports. Messrs Rendells and Sawdye, Auctioneers, conducted the sale of the livestock. Beatrice Chase, a local author, had a book stall at the Fair in the 1930s selling her own books. The Tug O' War competition was extended to competitors from any Parish in the county. The rules stated that no nails, irons, spikes or bars were allowed on the competitors' boots. Rain made it a very poor day and the afternoon sports had to be postponed. The Parish Council were asked to contribute some of the revenue from the side shows held on the Village Green to the running expenses of Widecombe Fair as there was a loss of £45.0s.0d.

1931 On Tuesday 8th September, the three fields behind The Old Inn were used for the Fair by kind permission of Mr. Broughton, landlord of The Old Inn. There is a photograph showing this in *The Western Morning News* of 9th September 1931. There was a large influx of visitors and a serious traffic problem. A report in the *Mid-Devon Advertiser* stated that thousands of people visited Widecombe

Judging children riders and ponies in the shadow of the famous church—the "Cathedral of the Moor."

Well Meadow (Site 4 on the Map)

on that day and that the Police and AA should be asked to help control the traffic in the following year. After two wet years, for the first time the Fair was insured against rain and it was a glorious day! There was an extraordinary slump in the sale of sheep and attendance of buyers was small with prices surprisingly low. 565 sheep were sent but only 208 were sold.

The Village Green was packed with stalls, cheap-jacks and fortune tellers.1931 was the first year that the cross-country race was held and Mr Keith Fox of Natsworthy presented a Cup for the winner. Frank Nosworthy, the local postman, won this race and that of the next two years, thus winning the Cup outright. The race is now known as the Uncle Tom Cobley Novelty Race and originally replaced the potato/ motor bicycle race. As the Tug O' War shield was won outright in the previous year by the Widecombe team, a new cup was presented by Captain Kitson. The 1931 Fair showed a loss of £27 and a sub-committee was formed to review the financial situation.

1932 Widecombe Fair Day was a local annual holiday. Committee Members were asked to pay an entrance fee to the Fair to help the financial position. 400 sheep were on offer but prices on average were £1 less than the previous year. It was remarked that "the Fair now seemed to be held in duplicate with the

48

visitors' attractions around the Village Green and, further down, 'the real fair' where a little business and a great deal of pleasure were mixed to great effect".

Many people had a great deal of difficulty leaving the village at the end of the day due to traffic problems. Evening entertainment was held in the large schoolroom in the upper storey of the Church House, comprising a selection of songs, readings and music. A donation from the revenue from the Fair was given to the Ashburton and Buckfastleigh Cottage Hospital.

Aerial view of the Fair, c 1932

1933 A rainy day after a long drought. This was the first year that stalls with a rural theme, such as handicrafts and country crafts, were allowed on the show field. Sheep were again penned on the grass adjoining the churchyard and 320 lots out of 400 were sold. It was at about this time that the Parish Council, as caretakers of the Village Green, began hiring out the site for side shows and stalls and the revenue received helped towards the running of the Parish. The Village Green was known in old times as Butts Park, the site of the ancient archery butts. **1934** It was suggested that Widecombe school children should have a holiday on Fair Day. Admission prices were one shilling for adults, six pence for children and one shilling and sixpence for cars. Some Committee Members agreed to

The Village on Fair Day 1933

take a collection around the village to raise funds and anyone donating ten shillings or more would have free admission to the Fair. Beatrice Chase, the local author, asked the BBC to broadcast the *Widecombe Fair* song on air, which may have contributed to the large attendance. A report in the *Mid Devon Advertiser* stated 'The Dartmoor farmers who had sheep to sell had every reason to be satisfied. Every one of the 445 Dartmoor ewes brought into the Fair changed hands, at an average price of 35s, an increase of seven shillings a head compared with last year. The top price was made by Mrs Norrish of Northway, who sold a pen at 44s.6d. per head to Mr G. Uglow of Tavistock. Mr Lee of North Bovey purchased a pen of two-teeth ewes from Mr W. Norrish of Tunhill at 41s.6d. Mr W. J. Mann, as usual, did not offer any of his prize ewes but 41 of his other sheep realised an average of 36s. Mr Jasper French of Southcombe sold forty at an average of 35s. Of the 21 rams offered twelve sold, the price ranging from £3 to £7.2s.6d. The highest figure was obtained for Mr W. J. Mann's first-prize ram, which was purchased by Mr Ball of Marytavy. Messrs Mortimore Bros (Hound Tor) gave five guineas for a ram offered by Mr G. Nosworthy. The auction was conducted by Messrs Rendell and Sawdye.'

As Frank Nosworthy had won the Cup for the Uncle Tom Cobley race three times, a new cup was presented to be known as the Keith Fox Perpetual Cup. This was again won by Frank Nosworthy. The 1934 Fair was visited by Sir Harry Lauder, notable Scottish entertainer of the time; he was appearing at the Palace Theatre, Plymouth. He sang the *Widecombe Fair* song with Uncle Tom Cobley (Edward Dunn), including a ninth verse recently found by Edward's sister in the Family Bible. Edward Dunn reputedly sold over 1000 signed photographs.

50

The Green on Fair Day 1934

SIR HARRY LAUDER paid a surprise visit yesterday to Widecombe Fair, and at the invitation of " Uncle Tom Cobley " took a " wee drappie " of Devonshire cider. — Western Morning News " Photo.

Harry Lauder meets Uncle Tom

:-: WIDECOMBE FAIR :-:

A great crowd of holidaymakers who attended the opening of the moorland village's celebrated Fair.

Happy children ride Uncle Tom's famous grey mare—a reminder of Jan Stewer, Bill Brewer, Peter Gurney, etc.

From the Express & Echo 1935

1935 The Chairman and Secretary were instructed to ask for tenders for the supply of draught and bottled beer, cider and mineral water on the fair ground. The Rising Sun Hotel, Torquay, tendered £4.4s.0d for the provision of a licensed marquee on the field. The Committee also agreed to accept a tender of £1 for the supply of ice cream. It was recorded that 'the picturesque Village Green was crowded with side shows and the usual paraphernalia of the Fairground, vendors of all kinds of articles from shaving brushes to clocks carried out a roaring trade'. *The Western Morning News* reported that 'The Fair ended somewhat prematurely and dismally in a downpour of rain. Unsuspecting holiday makers arrived unprepared and were caught 'in light summer apparel'. With hundreds of cars leaving the village simultaneously, there was much confusion of traffic and a number of blocks occurred on Widecombe Hill'.

Members of the Bournemouth Devonian Society attended the Fair.

1936 On the way to the Fair, eight buses and a score of other vehicles were held up as a gentleman walked through the heather to retrieve a hat blown from the head of a lady in the leading bus.

An open top bus.

Rendells & Sawdye and Mr Wakeham of Luscombe & Maye, South Brent, were asked to auction sheep at the Fair. 445 breeding ewes plus rams were sold. Mr Hill tendered the sum of £1 for supplying the teas. It was remarked that "It was not the moor folk that got the bad bargains from the cheap jacks – as they were content to watch the smart visitors from the towns match their wits against the sellers and enjoy the denouement".

A group of ladies from Plymouth arrived in the costume of Uncle Tom Cobley's friends and joined with him in the procession. The weather was cold with a wintry wind and occasional icy showers. Edward Dunn was very excited by an invitation to visit the USA – "Maybe I'll go next year".

It's thirsty work

1937 It was agreed at a committee meeting in 1937 that the Chairman should have a talk with the Police Sergeant to see if he thought it was necessary to employ a Constable on Fair day. Programmes were sold by the Scouts from Ashburton. The Widecombe Morris Dancers took part. The weather was again cold. Fewer than 200 sheep came under the auctioneer's hammer although prices were good.

Admission to the field cost one shilling and the programme threepence. The total receipts from the Fair in 1937 were £183.14s.11d and, once the bills were paid, the Treasurer expected the balance should be about £60, of which £40 was allotted for donations to charities. This sum was allocated as: £10 to the Nursing Association, £10 to the Blind Institute, £5 to the Village Hall, £5 to National Children's Homes and Orphanage, £5 to Bovey Tracey Hospital and £5 to Ashburton Hospital. This principle of donating to local, regional and national charities continues to the present time. Ten shillings was allocated to be distributed to the smaller children, given in coppers. This tradition developed over the years and, in time, a small cash gift was given to local children every year. Records show that the sum given in 1945 was one shilling, and this was raised by stages to two shillings and six pence, 50p in 1985, £1 in recent times and in 2006 the gift was in the sum of £2.00. The children receive tokens at school and then come to the committee tent on the day to receive their gift from the Treasurer.

1938 Following Edward Dunn's death, his second son, Robert, was offered £2 to act as Uncle Tom Cobley, if he was willing to sell programmes. The Ashburton Band were offered £8.8s.0d, provided they turned out at full strength. The weather was ideal but there was not a great number of sheep for sale. Mr W. J. Mann had retired from business and his famous flock had been dispersed. Many of the sheep normally sent to Widecombe Fair had changed hands at other fairs held beforehand. This was the last time sheep were sold at Widecombe Fair.

1939 Early in 1939, it was agreed to ask the Widecombe Bell Ringers to peal the bells from 10.30am until 11.30am on Fair Day and that a donation of ten shillings should be paid towards the Bellringers Outing Fund. Unfortunately, the 1939 Fair was subsequently cancelled due to the outbreak of World War II, the weather conditions being perfect.

QUIET WIDECOMBE

PERFECT WEATHER, BUT NO FAIR

Instead of being thick with crowds of people, rows of motor cars, coaches, stalls and pony and sheep pens, Widecombe slept peacefully in the moor on Tuesday in its usual calm. It was the day of the great country-famous Widecombe Fair, which had to be cancelled owing to the outbreak of war. At first it was decided to hold the sheep dog trials, but these had to be abondoned also.

It was a great blow to the villagers, to whom the Fair day is the outstanding day of the year, and the proprietors of the little curiosity shops were particularly disappointed.

What made the blow all the harder was that the weather conditions were perfect. The villagers could only gaze at the deserted Green and imagine the crowds of people who would be there enjoying the sun and the rural atmosphere of the fair.

A descendant of Uncle Tom Cobley, the old man who died recently and who had done so much to make Widecombe Fair the success it is, stood by a tattered bill advertising the fair, which shared a hoarding with an air raid precaution bill. He said several motorists and hikers had turned up during the day, thinking the fair was still on. Some of the cars bore London registration numbers. He was sure, however, that the fair would be started again as soon as the war was over. As he was speaking an aeroplane droned over the purple moorlands.

From the Mid Devon Advertiser 1939

1939 – 1944 A decision to cancel the 1939 fair was taken at very short notice at a meeting held on Tuesday, 5th September 1939, due to the outbreak of World War II. All village signs and the arms of signposts were removed during the war. In the process of removing the Widecombe Village sign which was decorated with coloured tiles, it was dropped and damaged beyond repair. During the period 1939 -1944 the Fair was not held. The sheep sale was moved to Ashburton and Chagford, never to return.

1945 A modified, and hastily organised fair was held after the end of hostilities. This consisted of children's races, gymkhana, sports and tug of war and all the profits of that fair (£104.1s.1d) were given to the 'Local Welcome Home Fund' for men and women who had served in the Forces. There were not many private cars due to petrol rationing and the committee decided that they were unable to provide teas owing to rationing and Ministry of Food restrictions. The three tea rooms in Widecombe were asked to give some of their profits to the Welcome Home Fund.

A new style of programme was produced with a picture of the grey mare on the cover and the song *Widecombe Fair* printed inside. Albert Dunn, the late Edward's third son, took over the role of Uncle Tom Cobley. Mr Bill Miners offered to bring his tractor along if the weather was wet to pull out cars disabled by wheelspin.

The War is over and the Fair is Back!

1946 Visitors to the fair totalled 2996. The entrance prices were two shillings and one shilling and a total profit of £183 was made. The Green was covered with stalls and side shows and the main attraction was, as usual, Uncle Tom Cobley with his whiskers and firkin of ale. Donations were made to Ashburton and Bovey Tracey charities.

1947 The first woman to run in the Uncle Tom Cobley race was Miss H. Barber, who took part with seven men. There was no sheep show, partly due to the severe blizzard in the previous winter which caused serious losses to farmers. There were ten horse and pony classes. Four championship cups were presented in these classes, together with a Hunting Crop for the best rider in Class 8.

A dance was held after the Fair and it was agreed to give the Ladies Committee who helped with the dance refreshments free admission to the gymkhana and show. It was also decided that free teas and other liquid refreshments were to be provided for members of the committee. Profits in 1947 were divided between Widecombe & District Nursing Association and the National Institute for the Blind.

1948 The grand daughter of Edward Dunn, Jean Nosworthy, aged 16, took part in the Uncle Tom Cobley race and finished a very creditable fourth. Following the

Fair, it was agreed to hold a dinner to which ladies would be invited. A BBC broadcast on *News of the Week* was criticised by the committee as being misleading. The general tone of the broadcast inferred that the Fair was run for the financial benefit of the village, whereas it was run for charity. The BBC was asked to set out the true facts.

In 1948 a new village sign depicting Uncle Tom Cobley and All was erected on the original granite base on its new site close to where the sheep sales were originally held. It was designed by Lady Sylvia Sayer and paid for by Mr F. Hamlyn of Dunstone Court.

1949 The show of sheep was reinstated after some years. The Fair was held in New Park, not on the Green. Bill Miners took the part of Uncle Tom Cobley and two girls took part in the downhill race, finishing 5th and 6th.

The New Village Sign 1948

Receipts for the New Village Sign. 1948.

Outside the Old Inn, 1949

1950 Police appealed to farmers for extra fields to be used as parking due to the immense volume of traffic. A tractor driving competition was introduced and Tom Hext took the part of Uncle Tom Cobley. Proceeds from the Fair were divided between Leusdon Church and St Dunstans for the Blind.

1951 Luncheon tickets were issued to the President, Chairman, Vice Chairman, Treasurer, three Secretaries and all Stewards and Judges. Jack Brown was the new Uncle Tom Cobley. There was again a tractor driving competition and later that evening a dance was held in the Parish Hall.

1952 It rained all morning but cleared up for the afternoon. Thereafter crowds flocked to the village, much to the jubilation of the committee members. Beatrice Chase later wrote that the weather had been the worst she could remember and stated "it was my proud lot to see Uncle Tom Cobley with his smock which I'd had made in Norfolk and presented to the Fair 24 years ago".

1953 One problem encountered this year was that Uncle Tom's firkin was so old it leaked. The traffic problem still needed to be resolved.

1954 A new traffic one-way system was introduced. On Fair day, two men ransacked Bittleford Farm and police searched for them amongst the crowd at the Fair.

1955 The Secretary was instructed to contact the Police and suggest that the one-way traffic system should be operated from midday until 6.00pm. A prize of £1 was offered for the first lady home in the Uncle Tom Cobley Race. Missing this year was Henry Charles, the Fairground operator, who had been renting the Green from the Parish Council for many years and who had been a stalwart of the Fair since a boy. His spinning jenny was brought by his son, Henry Junior, as it was his father's last wish.

1956 A two mile traffic jam on Widecombe Hill was caused by a broken down coach. Jack Brown, who took the part of Uncle Tom Cobley, was amazed at how many people asked him if his grey mare, Tidy, was the original mare.

1957 There was a large increase in the number of advertisements in the Fair programme – twenty one in all including Tuckers on the front cover. There were record numbers of sheep on show and record entries in the downhill race. One

of the beneficiaries of this year's Fair was the Restoration Fund for Widecombe's St Pancras Church (known as 'The Cathedral of the Moor'). The Fair was a major contributor to the Fund, which had the aim of raising £15,000. A note of the progress made for this Fund in the year may be of interest. At the beginning of April, the total amount raised stood at £3,129. To the date of the Fair an additional £754 had been raised. This had been done largely with the help of visitors to Widecombe to whom the Parish are very grateful.

1958 Among the events in 1958 were a Motor Cycle Rodeo and a Parade of the South Devon Foxhounds. A Royal Marine won the downhill race, the first and only time to date that a member of Her Majesty's Forces had achieved this feat. The RAC had a radio equipped mobile headquarters in the village.

Ned Northmore took the part of Uncle Tom Cobley, the first of twenty three occasions. Also for the first time, the Women's Institute made cakes and sold them in the Church House.

1959 The Royal Marines put on a Judo display and vehicles took part in an 'Old Crocks Race'. The person who came second in the Uncle Tom Cobley Race, Mr Jefferies, said he had run just for the fun of it and wished to hand his prize money of 30 shillings to the oldest person in Widecombe. This was Mrs Nosworthy who was ninety four, who told a reporter about her memories of the Fair. "The Fair used to be small with a few stalls selling sweets. There were a few sheep on the Village Green – that was long before the days of the private car. There were a few horses and carts but most people walked from outlying farms and came to the village for a great day out. The Fair is as good as it had ever been – different but just as good."

Carnival Float by the Royal Navy

Following a drought, supplies of beer, cider and minerals withstood enormous demand. Even washing up water was at a premium. In 1959, forty granite boulders were installed on the Green to protect it from erosion. Some of these boulders are rolled back each year to make easy access to the Green for fairground vehicles. The Church was undergoing restoration due to the ravages of death watch beetle and £50 was donated from the Fair's revenue.

1960 Ken Dodd visited the Fair. It was arranged for a Police Constable to be engaged for the day to avoid the trouble that arose in previous years by people getting from the car park into the Fair Field without payment. Harry Price presented a working model of Uncle Tom Cobley and All – a true to life model of seven men on the Old Grey Mare with 100 working parts. It was powered by the wheels and five of the riders moved their heads from side to side. (Where is it now?)

Russell Pearse, a local farm worker, beat off a strong challenge from the Royal Marines to win the downhill race. From the minutes it was discovered that 'more supervision over the chaos in the Committee Tent was required and someone should be asked to organise the system of free drinks'. The Tug O' War teams included Barnstaple Police, Plympton Police, ITC Lympstone, and the Royal Signals at Denbury. The Mary Tavy team won by beating off a challenge from the Chulmleigh team.

1961 Jimmy Jewel and Ben Warriss agreed to visit the fair and a cheque for ten guineas was presented to Ben Warriss in his capacity as 'King Rat' of the Grand Order of Water Rats.

A new grey mare Violet took part as the previous one, Tidy, 'took sick and died'. Violet was alarmed when a gas filled balloon was let off nearby but Ned Northmore (alias Uncle Tom Cobley) managed to stay mounted.

1962 The Motor Cycle Rodeo was replaced by a Sheep Dog demonstration. A Judo Display by the Royal Marines took place. Bryan Burdon, star of *Gaytime* at the Summer Pavilion in Paignton, opened the Gymkhana. *The Western Morning News* stated that 'there had been a Fair of some sort in Widecombe for 600 years though, for centuries, it had only been a sheep sale'. The fair showed a loss in 1962 of £117 due to bad weather – low cloud and continuous rain.

1963 The charge for a Police Constable to be in the Fairground for the day would have been £6.8s.0d. This was considered excessive and it was decided to erect barbed wire and posts instead to reduce unauthorised access. There was a Police Dog demonstration and the Local Hunt paraded their hounds. About 2000 people passed through the gate and many more came to see the village and the fun fair. There was a record entry of twenty six for the downhill race, fifteen of whom were Royal Marines. The Fair showed a profit of £59, of which £10.10s.0d was given to the Church Restoration Fund.

1964 In *The Guardian* dated 9th September 1964, the following report appeared: 'Uncle Tom Cobley, in the person of a local farmer, could only make it to Widecombe Fair on a gelding yesterday. They have been very short of grey mares on Dartmoor this year and a grey gelding was the nearest to the real thing the organising committee could produce. From late morning till early evening, the approach roads to the village were fumed up with cars and coaches.' (The beginning of global warming?) 'This led to a postponement of the sheepdog trials for an hour while the crowd waiting for the judge who was trapped in his van two miles back on the moor. It was the fair on the green which seemed to attract most attention. One woman, posing for a picture, complained bitterly that a monkey was biting her shoulder. Another woman wanted an Uncle Tom Cobley mug to take back for the children. "You can't" her husband replied ungenerously, "there is no such person. Have a toasting fork instead. It does not look so commercial."

There was a record number of thirty five competitors in the downhill race. Sadly, in 1964, it was a struggle financially to organise the Fair with heavy expenses before the day, but a profit of £243.15s.9d was made at the event.

1965 Following the resignation of Mr W. Miners from the committee, he offered a cup in memory of his years of service to the Fair. This is the W. F. Miners Perpetual Cup and was donated for the first lady home in the annual downhill race. Sideshows were beginning to appear in the Fair field. Bowling for a lamb was held instead of bowling for a pig. One newspaper report mentioned that Uncle Tom rode a grey gelding called 'Violet' – a confusion of gender!

A stretch of the imagination for the old grey mare.

1966 Rural art and craft demonstrations took place, such as thatching, rope making and spar stick making. Two displays were given by Bob Singleton of Bovey Tracey, the British champion axeman. The Tug O' War was reinstated after a lapse of a year or two. There was a big increase in expenditure and drop in income, thereby producing a profit of £108.3s.8d. Competitors as young as seven years took part in the downhill race but this would be reviewed in the next year. Funds were allocated to the Aberfan Disaster Fund and to Leusdon Memorial Hall.

1967 The Bishop of Crediton visited the fair and presented the cups. The local Vicar, the Reverend J. W. E. Brown, challenged the Bishop to a pillow fight and won. The Bishop said "If I had been in training, I would have beaten him". It was fought on a tree trunk about five foot above the ground and supported by what proved to be rather unsteady wooden posts. The 'pillows' were sacks of straw. A lower age limit of fourteen was introduced for the Uncle Tom Cobley Novelty Race. The Young Farmers' Club put on a demonstration and there was also a Wood Chopping competition.

1968 The Secretary promised to find a 'quieter band' for the evening dance! The use of colour printing in the programme was introduced. Owing to the cost, it was decided to abandon the Tug O' War but Donkey Racing was held in its place. Another pillow fight of note took place, this time between Jan Stewer and Uncle Tom Cobley, which Jan Stewer won. Brothers John and Mike Vooght took first and second places in the downhill race.

1969 Kathy Kirby, popular singer and entertainer, presented the cups at the Fair. She was appearing in Torquay at the time, and agreed to come to the Fair if the Committee would book a block of tickets for her show. This they did, at a cost of ten shillings to twelve shillings and six pence per ticket. Peter Kesteven, an artist from Newton Abbot, did pencil sketch portraits at five shillings a time and gave the proceeds of £4.10s.0d to the Widecombe Church Hall. 1969 was a record fair, with 3721 adults, 223 juveniles and 1319 cars. £130 was distributed to charities.

1970 Mayflower celebrations were taking place in Plymouth and 'Miss Mayflower' (Sandra Ritchie) attended the Fair, for a fee of two guineas. A replica of the Mayflower sailed from Plymouth to America this year. In the previous year, the organisers thought they had lost their celebrity when Kathy Kirby was held up in traffic. This time they gave the Police a description of the sports car bringing Miss Mayflower to the Fair but, anticipating hold-ups, she arrived in good time and was able to chat to Uncle Tom Cobley and have a ride on the grey mare before presenting the prizes. Due to poor weather the takings at the Fair were down and the profit was £57.16s.10d.

1971 This was the year when decimalisation of the currency was introduced and the entrance prices were therefore re-calculated at 15p per adult, 5p per

1969. Kathy Kirby judges the Fancy Dress Competition

child and car parking cost 35p or 15p. The cost of staging the Fair increased every year and, this year, £200 was spent on the prize money alone. Some visitors beat the expected traffic jams by arriving early and washing and shaving once they had found a ringside place. Leslie Crowther presented the cups at the Fair. £100 was available for distribution which was divided equally between the Church House, the Methodist Church Repair Fund at Dunstone, the British Empire Cancer Campaign and the Widecombe School Welfare Fund for netball equipment. A beat dance was held in the evening.

1972 In 1972, Dickie Henderson had been invited to visit the Fair but unfortunately the traffic that year was particularly bad and, by the time he arrived at Widecombe, he had to turn round and go straight back to Torquay to be in time for his performance at the Princess Theatre. A Donkey Derby took place again this year. The Marines promised thirty competitors for the Uncle Tom Cobley race. The race was won by Colin Pearse with his twin brother, James, in second place, possibly the only time twins have achieved this feat. The Fair was a great success with record numbers attending. Among the beneficiaries were Widecombe Parish Hall, Leusdon Memorial Hall for stage curtains and Widecombe Church Tower appeal.

1973 As usual, the local Hunts contributed to a parade. On various occasions over the years the South Devon Foxhounds, the Dartmoor Mink Hounds and the

North Dartmoor Beagles have attended. The organisers surprised the competitors in the downhill race by switching the start to the Bonehill side of the road and lengthening the route. The competitors were permitted to cross the road, but not run down it.

1974 Due to prolonged rain in the days leading up the Fair, an emergency committee meeting was called to consider whether the Fair should be cancelled. It was decided that the Fair should go ahead and that hardcore and land drains should be placed in the field. The Agricultural Secretary reported great difficulty with obtaining entries for the show classes that year. The biggest hazard for most people was not the traffic but wasps. Newton Abbot St John Ambulance were kept busy most of the day treating wasp stings. St John Ambulance have attended the Fair for many years.

1975 A Clay Pigeon shooting competition was organised by  The Meltor Gun Club. The galvanised iron shed in the Fair field was reported to be in a dangerous condition and it was agreed to demolish it. An American couple arranged their holiday to coincide with the Fair. The retired newspaper man and his wife had fallen in love with Dartmoor scenery, the Fair and the delicious Devonshire cream teas, and all of them had surpassed their expectations. A lady from Perth, Western Australia, Mrs May Dunstone came back for a holiday after thirty five years. She was thrilled to bits with the Fair and thought it was marvellous.

1976 A cup was donated for the first local person home in the Uncle Tom Cobley race in memory of Mr Frank Nosworthy. Mr Nosworthy, who died earlier in the year, was the first winner of the race in 1931 and also won the next three. There was a record entry in the race of thirty nine, eleven of which were girls. A Heavy Horse class was re-introduced this year. Among the charities benefiting were the National Institute for the Blind, Dr Barnardo's Homes and a sum was given for OAP Christmas presents in Widecombe and Leusdon.

1977 This was Queen Elizabeth II's Silver Jubilee year. To make the Jubilee Fair special, the organisers resurrected all the Widecombe Fair characters, so that Uncle Tom Cobley (Ned Northmore) was accompanied by: Bill Brewer (Jack Brown), Jan Stewer (Gordon Daw), Peter Gurney (James Legge), Peter Davy (John Gittins), Dan'l Whidden (Gerald Smerdon), Harry Hawk (Richard Pascoe).

The Newton Abbot Young Farmers' Club provided exhibitions of arts and crafts and livestock. The Village Green had been re-seeded in 1977 so a smaller selection of funfair attractions took place in the car park.

Silver Jubilee Programme

WIDECOMBE FAIR

celebrates the 25th Year of Reign
of
H.R.H. Queen Elizabeth II

  1952 1977

TO BE HELD IN THE OLD FIELD
(by arrangement with Miss Hamlyn and Mr. S. E. Northmore)

TUESDAY,
13TH SEPTEMBER, 1977

Programme 20p   Commence 10.30 a.m.

.... and All. 1977

1978 The Fair continued to draw large crowds and by 10.30am the car parks were full and there was still a queue on Widecombe Hill. Mr Lloyd Mortimore of Lizwell Farm, who was giving a sheep shearing demonstration, was left high and dry when the petrol feeding the generator for the clippers ran out. Uncle Tom came to the rescue – dashing to the Vicarage for a gallon of petrol kept for the Vicar's mower – and the demonstration continued. A very pleasing £600 was available for distribution. It was donated to the Widecombe Church House, Leusdon Memorial Hall, Dunstone Chapel, the Scanner Appeal, Guide Dogs for the Blind, Royal Airforce Benevolent Fund, the Cancer Campaign and two branches of the Riding for the Disabled.

There was a rumour going round that the original Uncle Tom had no intention of visiting Widecombe but went, in fact, to Whiddon Down. "This" said Tony Beard (the Wag from Widecombe) "was a load of rubbish. Uncle Tom definitely did go to Widecombe Fair. He would not have needed to borrow a mare to go to Whiddon Down but could have just hopped over the hedge of one of his fields."

1979 A first day commemorative cover was produced which was sold along with an article about the Fair. 5,000 of these were ordered. They could be sold at any time and placed under lock and key in Newton Abbot until 11th September, Fair Day, when they would be franked. In the event £800 profit was made on the postal covers. The cost of the postage was nine pence.

Over 5,000 people entered the Fair field – a record. By 12.30 all four car parks were jammed and the Fair Committee had to approach a local farmer for permission to use one of his fields to accommodate the vehicles still waiting to get in. The Secretary reported a wonderful day and an all time record. It was the first time in his memory that the programme of events kept to time.

Mrs Alchin at the Green Café felt that she could not undertake the Annual Dinner this year. As the committee felt that a Dinner outside Widecombe would not be supported, there was no Dinner.

WIDECOMBE FAIR

"*Widecombe Fair, Nobody there!*" was a rhyme I used to hear in the years before 1914. In those days the sheep were penned on the Green, and the rams were tied up near the churchyard wall, and almost the only stall was the one where an old lady sold "*fairings*"—very cheap and simple toys. After the First War village people came together to revive the Fair, and were so successful that nowadays we have to have one-way traffic for the day and fields made available as car parks for the hundreds of cars and coaches that bring the visitors. *How did it all begin?* Let us see first how it did *not* begin. The oldest Fairs in England are Charter Fairs, granted to noble landowners, usually for services rendered to the monarch, to whom the Fair was a useful source of revenue, so that even the most ancient were regularised by the grant of charters after the Norman Conquest. In 1889 the Government published a list of Fair Charters from 1200 to 1483 —Widecombe is not among them. Neither is there any mention of a Fair in the Parish Documents up to 1850. But in Volume 7 of the Parish Registers (Marriages 1813—1837) on the fly-leaf at the end of the book there is a note : "*Widecombe-in-the-Moor 25th Oct. 1850. We the undersigned were present at the First Fair this day established in this village, and dined with the Rev. H. Mason at the Vicarage House to celebrate the same as a Free Fair.*" Fourteen signatures follow beginning with the agent for the Lord of the Manor of Widecombe. Of the rest 5 are from Ashburton, 2 from Moreton—6 are farmers, 2 are solicitors, one is a butcher. No parishioners of Widecombe are among them. From 1851 there are small items for "*printing bills for the Fair*" "*for tarred cord for the Fair*", in the Vestry Book. For many years Widecombe Fair has been held on the 2nd Tuesday in September, and the old couplet might well be changed to : "*Widecombe Fair, Everyone there!*"

1980 The all-male Committee were desperately searching for a Secretary without success. Mrs Margaret Phipps volunteered to take the post and she was duly appointed. One member of the committee objected saying "but you're a woman!". She was not elected on to the Committee until 1984. Two complimentary Dinner tickets were sent to Mrs Christine Lamb in appreciation of her kindness in making a new smock for Uncle Tom Cobley.

1981 The Uncle Tom Cobley race was won by Christine Slade – the first and only time to date it has been won by a woman. By doing this, Christine won three trophies, those for, the winner, the first lady and the first local. A Log Axing competition took place. The Tug O' War was again revived after a few years lapse. Admission charges were £1 to the car park and 50p and 25p entrance to the field. 1981 was the last year that Ned Northmore portrayed Uncle Tom Cobley after twenty four years in the role.

1982 Local children were encouraged to compete in four classes. Wild flowers in an unusual container, an animal made from a vegetable, junk art and a painting of the Fair. This proved so popular that the Widecombe Primary School children continue to partake in various activities to this day including Maypole Dancing demonstrations and an exhibition of craft work. The local Royal British Legion donated a cup for the child gaining the most points in the children's classes.

Details were received of an old Widecombe Fair cup which had turned up in a second hand shop in Brixham. It was the Natsworthy cup, last won in 1952. It was purchased by the committee for £55 and it was decided to use it for the 1983 Fair for the Pedestrian Fancy Dress.

Gordon Daw took over the role of Uncle Tom Cobley. A sheep shearing demonstration took place. The Reverend John Brown presented the committee with the bell from his back door. It had been used by the Fair for many years for starting the Show Jumping. A valuation of the trophies by Ham & Huddy revealed a value of £3,111.

£750 revenue from the Fair was allocated, amongst others to Widecombe School, Rowcroft Hospice, Riding for the Disabled and the South Atlantic Fund (for the troops who fought in the Falklands' War).

It was reported in the Minutes of August 1982, that a ballot had been taken regarding the Widecombe Fair Dinner. Members of the Committee were asked which of two venues (Dartmeet and the Green Café) should be used and whether they would attend. Twenty five ballot papers were returned. Twenty voted for Dartmeet, of which sixteen would go and four didn't know. Five voted for the Green Café, of which three would go and two would not! The Dinner was therefore held at Dartmeet on 7th October.

1983 The question of the Tom Cobley trade mark was discussed by the committee. A letter from a solicitor was read to the effect that it would be difficult to enforce a copyright to belong to the Fair Committee which could not be used by the general public.

Mr Richard Frost agreed to do a horse shoeing demonstration at the Fair. It

was also decided to have a few old tractors and machinery on display. It was learned that Miss M. Hamlyn, the owner of the Fair field, was intending to change the ownership to one of her relations, but would give the Widecombe Fair Committee the right to hold the Fair in that field every year in the future. It was agreed to approach Miss Hamlyn to see if she would sell the field to the Widecombe Fair Committee.

In October 1983, a set of stamps was issued by the Post Office depicting Fairs, one of which was Widecombe Fair.

Miss Hamlyn once again supporting the Fair

1984 Miss Hamlyn gave the Fair Committee the chance to buy New Park as she wished to see Widecombe Fair continue in the future. The price was £11,000. The decision to buy the field was carried with fourteen votes for and one against. Four members were chosen to act as Trustees for the Committee in the purchase. Mr Simon Northmore (Ned) made a generous gift of £2,000 towards the purchase of New Park and an anonymous gift for £500 was also received.

Bass Brewery Shire Horses

The special attraction was the Bass Brewery Shire Horse team. The children at Widecombe School produced the biggest entry so far in the Children's Competitions. The classes were for a wild flower arrangement in an unusual container and a painting to do with the Fair. Six stalls were allowed on the field and a demonstration of hand chime ringing was given by Moretonhampstead school children. Takings at the Fair were £3,399, producing a profit of £1,800.

1985 *The Western Morning News* reported that the Fair was 'going from strength to strength with thirty four trophies and many special prizes available'. A first this year was an exhibit of high quality craft work. Local children were again presented with tickets to enable them to claim 50p, from the Committee. This tradition continues to the present day.

1986 All the pupils at Widecombe School entered the Children's Competition. The Police were allowed to use the school playground for parking. There was a parade of Horses and Carriages.

Due to Gordon Daw's retirement from the role of Uncle Tom Cobley, Peter Hicks took over, the first of eleven occasions. A cup for the best local Tug O' War team was presented by the family in memory of Mr Ern Avery (Bungy). A silver salver was received in memory of the late Miss M. Hamlyn and, due to her interest in Dartmoor ponies, it would be presented to the person gaining the most points in the Dartmoor pony classes.

A newspaper reporter told of an incident on the Green. "Before we leave Widecombe, I must tell you about a market stallholder I spotted there who, I fear, must have been new to the business. He seemed to be losing his patience with a particular customer's inability to see what a bargain an imitation marble table he had for sale was. "Oh, you want me to knock something off do you?" he asked. There was a wrenching noise then he added "There I've knocked one of the legs off for you."

1987 In May an article was published by the British Tourist Board in the *Weekend Australian*. An extract states 'The song did it of course. Without that rollicking Victorian baritone ditty about the seven – Bill Brewer, Jan Stewer, Peter Gurney, Peter Davey, Dan'l Whiddon, 'arry 'awk and Uncle Tom Cobley and all – who borrowed Tom Pearce's grey mare to go to Widecombe Fair, the village of Widecombe-in-the-Moor might never see a touring party all summer long.' Who knows?

In 1987, planning permission was granted for permanent toilets, the facilities before that being somewhat primitive. Pillow fighting was held, along with twenty three sheep classes (100 entries) and three Show Jumping classes. There were also over 100 entries in the 17 horse and pony classes. Churchwarden and supporter of Widecombe Fair, Miss Sylvia Needham, presented the prizes. Miss Needham (a breeder of South Devon cattle and Whitefaced Dartmoor Sheep) had participated in the Fair for many years, as an exhibitor and a judge.

1988 A Family Dog Show was introduced and this has remained extremely popular ever since. Also introduced this year were vegetable classes for local people which also proved very popular. The Produce Marquee continues to be a very popular attraction. Over forty cups and trophies were presented. Visitors remarked on the 'wonderful array of silverware for a one day show'.

Building work on the new toilets was carried out with Committee members helping when possible. By December the costs were £4,914, and doors, fencing and tree planting were still to be done.

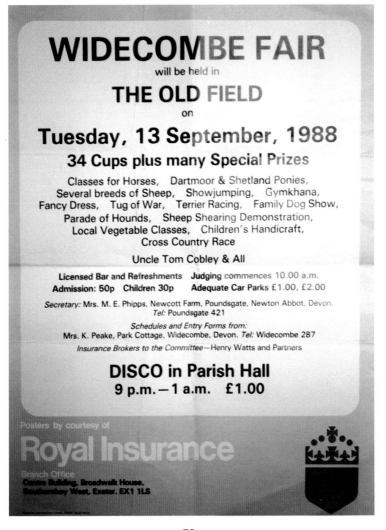

WIDECOMBE FAIR
will be held in
THE OLD FIELD
on
Tuesday, 13 September, 1988
34 Cups plus many Special Prizes

Classes for Horses, Dartmoor & Shetland Ponies,
Several breeds of Sheep, Showjumping, Gymkhana,
Fancy Dress, Tug of War, Terrier Racing, Family Dog Show,
Parade of Hounds, Sheep Shearing Demonstration,
Local Vegetable Classes, Children's Handicraft,
Cross Country Race

Uncle Tom Cobley & All

Licensed Bar and Refreshments   Judging commences 10.00 a.m.
Admission: 50p   Children 30p   Adequate Car Parks £1.00, £2.00

Secretary: Mrs. M. E. Phipps, Newcott Farm, Poundsgate, Newton Abbot, Devon.
Tel: Poundsgate 421

Schedules and Entry Forms from:
Mrs. K. Peake, Park Cottage, Widecombe, Devon. Tel: Widecombe 287

Insurance Brokers to the Committee—Henry Watts and Partners

DISCO in Parish Hall
9 p.m.—1 a.m.   £1.00

Posters by courtesy of
Royal Insurance
Branch Office
Centre Building, Broadwalk House,
Southernhay West, Exeter. EX1 1LS

1989 The pony classes were cancelled at the last minute due to an outbreak of Equine Flu. Terrier racing came into its own with extra events and they have continued to be part of the fair ever since. Despite the lack of ponies, £3,000 was raised for charity. The front cover of the programme was redesigned, incorporating a copy of the Village Sign. Before that the Widecombe Fair logo had been used. There were also many more advertisements.

Despite the inclement weather, an aerial display took place which was sponsored by Television South West who also sponsored the Uncle Tom Cobley race. The Secretary reported that the Fair had developed over the last ten years to include produce classes, children's handicrafts, stands of all kinds including old and new machinery. The Treasurer reported a profit of £3,036.80, some of which would be put aside for repairs to the fence, some deposited to cover next year's Fair and the remainder was to be donated to ten charities. It was proposed that the term 'local' for entries in the Fair was extended to include Postbridge.

Jimmy Frost from Buckfastleigh, won the Grand National this year on Little Polveir. Jimmy, a National Hunt jockey, had ridden at Widecombe Fair for many years and donated a cup in 1975, the Blue Grass Memorial Cup, in memory of his outstanding gymkhana horse Blue Grass.

1990 This year was a fine example of how the weather can affect the Show. Brilliant weather contributed to a 100% increase in takings. Due to the popularity of the produce classes, extra space and tables were allocated. A well kept secret was that the grey mare was pregnant. The TV celebrity, Trevor Appleton, visited the Fair and there was, once again, a parade of three packs of hounds.

1991 A quotation taken from the *Sunday Express* dated 15th September stated 'to organise a Fair of this kind is rather like going on an ocean voyage when your only navigation aid is a bailing bucket and your crew is in a constant state of mutiny'. Over 6,000 visitors attended the Fair. There was a parade of horses and carriages. In a change of venue the evening disco was held on the Fair field. Together with the Tug 'O War, it was hoped to provide continuous on-field entertainment right through to midnight.

1992 A new post of Honorary Life President was created for Mr Jim Hine in recognition of his past services to the Fair. A painting was commissioned as a gift for him which was painted by Mr Michael Smerdon who, in 2004, became Chairman of the Committee. On 8th June 1992, The Widecombe Fair Committee formed themselves into a Limited Company, to be known as The Widecombe Fair Committee Co Ltd. It was agreed that Committee meetings should, in future, be held on the second Tuesday of each month.

£3,550 was distributed to charities and various organisations including Guide Dogs for the Blind, Princetown Scouts, Widecombe School, Citizen's Advice

View from the Church Tower

Bureau, Princetown School, South West Children's Hospice and a sum was set aside for the relaying of the path at Widecombe Church.

1993 The Ashburton and South Dartmoor Journal reported that 'the Uncle Tom Cobley impersonator for the last eight years has been Peter Hicks. He wore the traditional top hat which was made in 1862. The hat is rather bent and fragile and slightly green.' Peter sported his own beard which he later had shaved off for charity and made over £600. A plan of the field appeared in the programme. There was also a Ladies' Side Saddle display and a parsnip entered by Percy Bishop was recorded as being over twenty eight inches long.

Terry Wogan sang the famous song and plugged the Fair on his early morning radio show. A group of riders raising funds for Riding for the Disabled rode from Sticklepath to Widecombe Fair to raise funds for their organisation. Cheques were presented on the day to the Guide Dogs for the Blind and Children's Hospice SW.

1994 In an effort to ease the traffic flow, a new one-way system was set up which only allowed coaches, HGVs and horse boxes down Widecombe Hill. Cars were directed by another route.

Henry Watts retired as Secretary and was succeeded by Mike Sutherland Cook. The Bale Tossing Competition was held for the first time. Two local walks were included in the programme. The Committee agreed to sponsor a local man, Mark Hutchins, to the sum of £100 to represent England in the Tug O' War competition National Finals.

1995 A new trophy (the Joan Perkins Perpetual Cup) was given to the Fair Committee for the best local vegetable. It was won this year by Caroline Mann. A new event introduced was Ferret Racing and Widecombe Play Group ran a cow-pat competition. A plan of the village was printed in the programme. Unfortunately, a generator belonging to E. Bowden & Son was stolen from the field, which cost the Fair Committee a large sum in compensation, thus reducing the profit for the year.

1996 Sarah Nosworthy and Sarah Mortimore decided to re-enact the reputed journey from Spreyton to Widecombe on horseback. They completed the journey in one hour and seventeen minutes, not bad for a seventeen mile ride. Details of their route appear earlier in this book.

There were displays of vintage machinery, sheep shearing, thatching and over twenty stalls of rural crafts, local produce, hand made clothing, wrought iron work, local artists and dried flowers. Over 10,000 people attended the Fair. The refreshment stall on the Fair field (run by the Old Inn) served 1000 bacon rolls, 400 gallons of beer and 1,150 cups of tea. The Widecombe Fair Committee was able to donate £5,500 to local and national charities, much to the delight of the organising committee.

Children's Riding Classes

1997 Richard Frost, who had been the Farrier for twenty five years, was presented with a granite plaque to commemorate his exceptional service to the Fair. Ben Deeble took on the post of Farrier and also won the downhill race for the fifth time. Ben's father, Tony Deeble, took on the role of Uncle Tom Cobley following Peter Hicks's retirement. Tony described himself as the first cockney to be Uncle Tom.

The cover of the programme was printed in colour, including a photograph of Uncle Tom Cobley on the front. It was decided that each year the Committee would adopt a charity to be the principal beneficiary of the Fair's donations. They would be supplied with a free stand on the field.

1998 The children of Widecombe School provided a display of country dancing. The crowd were as usual entertained by the Widecombe Wag, Tony Beard. Few of them knew that he was suffering from a fractured ankle, the result of being kicked by a cow. A new attraction was the fancy dress competition for dogs, part

Lunch at the Fair

of the extremely popular Family Dog Show. Geoffrey Bamsey took over as Secretary to the Committee. Attendance was severely affected by bad weather. Despite this a donation of £1,000 was made to the Widecombe Parish Church, of St Pancras, which was running an appeal to raise over £100,000 for repairs to the 130 foot church tower.

1999 Admission to the field cost £2, children 50p. Once again, local school children enthralled the visitors (many of whom joined in) with a demonstration of Maypole dancing. The Women's Institute celebrated their 50th birthday by doing light lunches and cream teas in the Church House to help their funds. Local postman, Mike Leaman, was on the field raising sponsorship for a charity bike ride over the Himalayas in aid of Mencap. He completed 250 miles in ten days on a standard issue three-speed postal bike.

The South Western Electricity Board supplied mains electricity to the Fair field free of charge and donated four days power in return for free publicity in the

2001. Foot and Mouth outbreak

Ross and Lupin. 2002

programme. As a result of an exceptional year, £6,733 was donated to charity, the principal donation being £4,000 to the Widecombe Church Tower Appeal.

2000 The Widecombe Fair Committee provided a display at the Flower Festival in the Church in June. Industrial action affected petrol supplies this year, which resulted in an attendance of only 3,500 in spite of it being a glorious day and those who got there thoroughly enjoyed themselves. The losers were those who decided not to attend. One person not affected by the fuel shortage was Uncle Tom who arrived on time on his grey mare.

Ned Northmore died earlier in the year and a new trophy was donated in his memory by the Committee for the Champion Whitefaced Dartmoor Sheep. George Southcombe donated the Herbie trophy for the best local lead rein pony in memory of his pony Herbie who had attended many Fairs, ridden by many different children. A Sheep Dog demonstration was once again featured. For the first time, a Town Criers' competition took place in the Village Square. Later the Criers joined the Grand Parade in the Fair field – a very colourful addition. This has continued to date.

2001 The fair was cancelled due to the outbreak of Foot and Mouth Disease. The date (11th September) became notorious due to the terrorist attacks on the Twin Towers of the World Trade Centre in America and is subsequently known as 9/11.

2002 A fine day. Sheep were absent from the Fair due to Foot and Mouth regulations. There was a display of birds of prey by Dartmoor Hawking and a demonstration of Working Shire Horses (Ross and Lupin) by Annie Williams. Morris Dancing took place in the evening. The Dartmoor Pony Society, with the Rare Breeds Survival Trust, had a stand outlining their work.

Beneficiaries were Sense, Mencap, Widecombe Playgroup, Rowcroft Hospice and the Parish Link. In May, The Widecombe Fair Committee Co Ltd purchased Great Close, 9.29 acres adjoining the Fair field, which secured the ownership of the main car park.

2003 In a change to the charging structure, car parking fees were discontinued. There was a new class in the pony show for a Veteran Horse or Pony over twenty years of age and the Routley Shield was presented to the winner. After about thirty years this was the last year for show jumping.

Pam St Clements, who takes the part of Pat Butcher in the BBC soap, *Eastenders*, and who has had a long standing connection with the Parish since childhood, judged the Fancy Dress competition. Tracey Elliot-Reep did a sponsored ride from John O' Groats to Lands End in aid of Riding for the Disabled. She began the ride on 18th July and called in at the Field on Fair day, before continuing to Land's End.

2004 A Park and Ride scheme was introduced with a mini-bus running from Southcombe Hill to the Fair field. This proved invaluable and was well used. For the first time, a Dartmoor Hill Pony Championship was held, confined to ponies bred on the moor.

This year's chosen charity was the Teignbridge branch of the Multiple Sclerosis Society. In contrast to a traditional sheepdog demonstration, a display of how ducks can be controlled by dogs was given. Also appearing were a Jester and a Mountain Bike display. The Dartmoor National Park Authority was promoting an oral history project collecting recorded memories of the Moor from local people. The Project Officer said that there used to be fairs and markets in every village on Dartmoor but these are becoming fewer. They are very important for the cultural heritage of the Moor.

School tribute to Peter Hirst

At the Fair's annual dinner in October of this year the Chairman, Peter Hirst, collapsed and died. He was also an active member of The Widecombe History Group and supported Widecombe School. At his funeral a collection was made and the money was used to purchase the material for the children to create the above mosaic in his memory.

2005 A display of Dog Agility was given by the South Hams Dog Agility Group. There was a display of vintage machinery and two of Brian Harris's lorries in their green and red livery. One of these lorries was driven every Sunday, between 1989 and 2001, from Crediton in Devon to Dundee in Scotland carrying UHT milk, an estimated total distance of 1½ million miles.

The Widecombe and District Local History Group were invited to provide an exhibition in a Heritage Marquee. There were displays and photographs of Ponsworthy, Widecombe Fair and North Hall, together with old farming tools. The Group had produced some paperweights, made from the lead salvaged from the Church Tower in 2001, and these were sold as souvenirs along with various Group publications. The tent was shared with Colin Pearse and the Devon Farms Holiday Accommodation Group. Colin Pearse launched his book *The Whitefaced Drift of Dartmoor's 'prapper' Sheep* giving a history of the Widecombe Whitefaced Dartmoor Sheep (the Widecombes).

One of the charities to benefit from the Fair was the Cavitron Fund at Derriford Hospital in Plymouth, which provides equipment for the treatment of brain cancer.

Outside the Heritage Tent

2006 This was a record breaking Fair, both in numbers and takings. For the first time for many years South Devon cattle were on show, and also alpacas. A hot air balloon was launched in the evening from the Fair field into a very misty sky. In an amazing coincidence it landed at Spreyton (Ham Farm). Spreyton was where the infamous ride started on the grey mare all those years ago.

As a result of the success of the Heritage Marquee in 2005, the Local History Group were invited to take part again and the occasion was used to launch their new publication *One Hundred Years and More of Ponsworthy*. Much interest was expressed in the copies of the Census from 1841 to 1901 and many visitors spent time looking at them. Information was gathered from visitors for use in this book.

The Devon Air Ambulance (which Widecombe Fair has continually supported) was called out to take a young child to hospital. An instant collection was made on the Fair field which raised a considerable sum. The helicopter landed in South Meadow, adjacent to the school, one of the former sites of the Fair.

Taking off for Spreyton

The launch of the Ponsworthy book

During the year a metal detector was used to search the Fair field and a 1797 'Cartwheel' Penny was found. Cartwheel pennies were minted for the British Government and were named 'Cartwheels' because of their not inconsiderable size.

Cartwheel Penny found on the Fair Field

2007 The Widecombe and District Local History Group celebrated its tenth anniversary with the publication of this book.

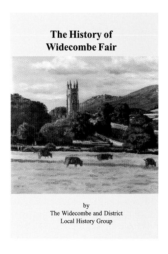

UNCLE TOM COBLEY IMPERSONATORS

1928 – 1937	Edward Dunn. Sometimes quoted incorrectly as John, Tom or James.
1938	Robert Dunn. Second son Edward Dunn.
1939 – 1944	Widecombe Fair cancelled due to outbreak of World War II.
1945 – 1948	Albert (Bert) Dunn. Third son of Edward Dunn.
1949	William (Bill) Miners.
1950	Tom Hext.
1951 – 1957	Jack Brown.
1958 – 1981	Simon (Ned) Northmore.
1982 - 1985	Gordon Daw.
1986 – 1996	Peter Hicks.
1997 - 2000	Tony Deeble.
2001	Cancelled due to Foot & Mouth disease.
2002 to date	Tony Deeble.

In other chapters of this publication the reader can find the legend, story, family tree and other details of The Uncle Tom Cobley who visited Widecombe Fair all those years ago. There is also a chapter dedicated to the various renditions of The Widecombe Fair song. In this chapter we look at the people that have portrayed Uncle Tom Cobley at the Fair since 1928.

It all started with a suggestion from Beatrice Chase, (Olive Katharine Parr) the authoress who came to Venton, in the parish of Widecombe in about 1900. She lived before that in London and, due to ill health, her mother was advised to take her to a south coast health resort. They went to Dawlish, but Beatrice's health did not improve. A lady there told her mother to "Get her out to Dartmoor while there is still time". She moved to Dartmoor with her mother Katharine Parr, who incidentally claimed to be a descendant of Katharine Parr (one of the wives of Henry the Eighth). Beatrice became a well known authoress and published many books with a Dartmoor flavour.

Beatrice Chase.

In 1928 Beatrice Chase suggested to a local farmer, Edward Dunn, that he ought to dress up as Uncle Tom Cobley. She provided him with a smock and so the portrayal of Uncle Tom Cobley became a regular feature of the Fair. She also gave Edward a traditional cider 'Keg' which he always carried with him and, with his own whiskers and top hat, he really looked and played the part. In one of her books, from 1948, she relates "I am proud to say it was I, years ago, who started the Old Uncle Tom Cobley procession, by presenting a genuine smock frock from Norfolk to Mr Dunn. This gave him the idea of impersonating that famous gentleman and now his son, Mr Albert Dunn, carries on the tradition and does it splendidly".

Let us now look at those who have portrayed Uncle Tom Cobley in some detail:-

EDWARD DUNN

He was the first man to take the part of Uncle Tom Cobley at Widecombe Fair. He was encouraged to take up the role by Beatrice Chase. He played the role from its instigation in 1928 until his death in early 1938 at the age of 67.

Edward Dunn

Edward was born in North Devon but moved to Somerset where he married. He and his wife had eight children, four boys and four girls. Two of his sons, Robert and Albert, followed in his footsteps by playing the part of Uncle Tom Cobley. In 1924 he moved with his family to Widecombe where they lived in Stouts Cottage. He worked at The Old Inn and later moved to Dunstone House.

He did much to re-establish the fame of Uncle Tom Cobley and was a wonderful attraction on Fair days with his faithful dog Ben in close attendance. It was however not only on Fair days that he portrayed the role and during the summer months he could be found on the Village Green suitably attired. He was a great self-publicist and charged money for his autograph. He signed many thousands so probably made quite a tidy living from this alone. He also charged to have his photograph taken and would allow people to sit on the old grey mare for which there was a further charge. In this way he supplemented his income to great effect. He was also involved in the creation of a series of postcards illustrating the Widecombe Fair Song, with some of his friends taking the parts of the characters.

Folklore says he died chopping wood but Jean Nosworthy, his granddaughter, says he was going out into a field behind Dunstone House with her and her brother, William, when he collapsed and died.

In interviews with *The Western Morning News* in 1934 and 1936, he made various claims, most of which cannot be substantiated:-

He said his sister, who lived in North Devon, had found a new verse to the famous Widecombe song. It was in a family bible and hitherto had been unpublished and unsung. He also claimed to be a direct descendant of Tom Cobley, the Cobleys and the Dunns having intermarried. He said he had had a farm in North Devon but had, some ten years previously (1924), given it up to and come to Widecombe where he had trained his horse in the role of the old grey mare which she now had off to perfection.

He claimed to have been shown all over the world due to the film *Escape* made in 1929 on Dartmoor. He was he said very famous in the USA and was being urged to go out there for a promotional tour. His dog, Ben, was also in the film, so he said. He claimed to have been made a member of The Society of Authors for his work and for making Dartmoor immortal.

ROBERT DUNN

Second son of Edward Dunn, he took up the role after the death of his father and at the request of the Widecombe Fair Committee. His elder brother William had emigrated to Canada. However, he played the role only once in 1938. As he lived in Rockbeare he came back to Widecombe for the day just so the family tradition could be carried on. The outbreak of World War II in 1939 caused the cancellation of the Fair until 1945.

Robert Dunn

86

ALBERT DUNN

Albert was the third son of Edward Dunn and brother of Robert. Jean Nosworthy relates that at the 1945 Fair there was a bit of a confrontation between Robert and Albert as to who should be riding the old grey mare. It is believed that the Fair organisers had asked Albert to take the role as he still lived in the Parish. He continued the family connection with the role of Uncle Tom Cobley from 1945 to 1948 a total of four times.

WILLIAM (BILL) MINERS

Bill only played the role once - in 1949, offering his services for the role when it was decided to have a change from a member of the Dunn family.

Bill's father walked from Holsworthy to Widecombe in 1902 or 1903 looking for work

Albert (Bert) Dunn

on a farm. It is understood that he finally obtained work at Lizwell where his family joined him. They all lived at Windwhistle Cottage.

He subsequently got a job working for the Council repairing roads and he was reputedly involved in the making of a track into Dipleigh in about 1921. It was

Bill Miners

there that he met his future wife, Olive Collins, who came from Stoke Gabriel, and worked as a maid at Dipleigh. They were married and produced nine children.

Bill started a haulage firm using a horse and cart and in 1927 bought his first lorry. He and his brother Sam were in partnership but later went their separate ways. Bill had his sons, Freddy and Bernard, working with him and W. F. Miners & Sons was born. The business grew and its depot moved to Ashburton.

He was very community spirited and did much to get electricity to Widecombe. He was also passionate about bell ringing and was captain of the tower for years. He is remembered each August with a bell ringing competition for the W. Miners Rose Bowl. He was Chairman of the Parish Council and in

1950 was Chairman of the Fair's organising committee. As a young man he was an enthusiastic athlete and ran in races all over the county. He was also a member and later coach to the local tug of war team. His connection with the Fair lives on due to the presentation of a cup W. F. Miners Perpetual Challenge Cup to the first lady home in the annual Uncle Tom Cobley Novelty Race.

TOM HEXT

Tom only performed the role once in 1950 when he was 76 years old. He had no need of a false beard as he grew his own but he wore the traditional smock.

He was a bachelor who was born at Hatchwell in Widecombe. He spent much of his life working for various farmers, householders and other businesses doing agricultural work and gardening.

He was known affectionately as Uncle Tom Hext to a great many people of the district and was a real character, full of fun, and a real wit. He acquired the nickname of 'Peewit' due to his ability to imitate the call of the Lapwing. He was also able to imitate the calls of various other birds, often confusing people by doing bird calls out of season. Tom died three years later, in 1953, at the age of 78 and is buried in Leusdon churchyard.

Tom Hext

JOHN (JACK) BROWN

John was known to most people as Jack and performed the role of Uncle

Tom Cobley on seven occasions between 1951 and 1957. He had a pleasant way of chatting to the visitors on Fair Day and was fascinating to talk to with a warm personality.

He was born in Beaworthy, North Devon where he married Florence Knight, also of Beaworthy, in about 1920. Together they produced eleven children, six sons and five daughters. The family moved from Beaworthy to Canna in North Bovey, and then to Broadhempston. In about 1928 they moved to Dockwell Farm, Widecombe, but due to his employer getting married they then moved on to Tremills at Lower Dunstone where he lived for the rest of his life. It was a

Jack Brown

friendly home and open to all who passed by for a chat and a bite to eat. Jack had a grey mare which he rode to work at Dockwell. Later in life he gave up farm work and was employed by Gerry Harris on the lorries.

He and his family did a great deal for the parish and took a keen interest in local affairs. The last of his children left Widecombe in 2005 but still keeps an interest in the parish.

Those who knew 'Father Brown' as he was affectionately known found him to be a very interesting man to talk to who had a wealth of country stories to tell. He was well liked and never had a bad word to say about anyone. He died in 1981 at the age of 83 and is buried in Widecombe churchyard.

SIMON (NED) NORTHMORE

Ned took the part of Uncle Tom Cobley on twenty-four occasions from 1958 to 1981 and therefore performed the role more than anyone else to date. He was

Ned Northmore

born at Yellowmead, Sheepstor, in 1916. Later the family moved to Glebe Farm, Woodleigh and later still to Pollards Coombe in the parish of Slapton in South Devon. The family moved to Mill Leat, Holne in the 1920s and moved again to Kingshead, Widecombe, in about 1937. Both his parents died there and are buried in Widecombe churchyard.

Ned married Lillian, a lady's maid, who was known locally as Cissie, during World War II but there were no children from the marriage. Ned often said that they married quickly as Lillian was in imminent danger of being called up for service in the armed forces. He continued to farm Kingshead until his retirement. They then moved to Stoanen, a cottage overlooking Widecombe Village Green.

Both Ned and his wife were tireless workers for the parish supporting all village events. Ned was a churchwarden for over fifty years and treasured a letter of congratulation from the Archbishop of Canterbury. He bred South Devon cattle and Whitefaced Dartmoor Sheep and was on the Widecombe Fair organising committee. His association with the Fair is marked by the Ned Northmore Perpetual Memorial Trophy given each year for the champion Whitefaced Dartmoor Sheep.

Ned will be remembered with a great deal of affection by all who knew him. He and his wife are buried in Widecombe churchyard.

GORDON DAW

Gordon performed the role four times from 1982 to 1985. His two sons-in-law took the parts of two of Uncle Tom's travelling companions. He was born at Natsworthy Farm, Widecombe in 1921, where his father was farming. When his father died Gordon continued farming there until his retirement in 1985. He was a local man through and through and a great supporter of Widecombe Fair. He could remember when sheep were penned and sold on the Village Green – a practice which came to an end in 1939 at the start of World War II.

Gordon's father won prizes for heavy horses and Gordon carried on the tradition by showing Dartmoor Ponies. He won the Colonel Hankey Cup for the best brood mare from 1934 to 1936 and therefore won it *Gordon Daw* outright. He treasured it for the rest of his life.

He was a countryman and took great pleasure in following the local hunt. He died in Widecombe in 2006 and is buried in Widecombe churchyard.

PETER HICKS

Peter performed the role of Uncle Tom Cobley eleven times from 1986 to 1996. He was born on 13th October 1932 and was the fourth child and only son of Samuel and Winifred Hicks of Balls Farm, Daccombe, near Kingskerswell. The family moved to Higher Venton, Widecombe in March 1948. Beatrice Chase then owned the farm and, upon her death in 1955, Peter inherited the farm.

In 1960 Peter married Betty Irish a local girl and they have two daughters. Peter and Betty still live at Venton.

Peter became involved in village life soon after arriving in Widecombe, this despite being told by his father to "keep his eyes open and his mouth shut". He became part of the Widecombe Fair Committee and was its Agricultural Secretary for seven years and *Peter Hicks* its Chairman for six years.

Peter's father had a grey mare called Tidy, which was ridden on Fair day by both Gordon Daw and Jack Brown when they were portraying the role.

Widecombe Church and the Parish Council have also been part of Peter's life. In 1996 Peter had a booklet published about his role as Uncle Tom Cobley, Widecombe Fair and his personal life.

TONY DEEBLE

Tony has performed the role since 1997 a total of nine times. There was no Fair in 2001 due to the Foot & Mouth epidemic. He does not have to wear a false beard as he sports his own whiskers.

He originates from London's Notting Hill and professes to be a cockney. He left London and came to Dartmoor in 1983. He was a tree surgeon but now works for a local machinery firm and lives at Challacombe.

He has managed to pick up the local dialect rather well but doesn't drink the local brew of scrumpy (cider) preferring lager instead. For many years he has taken part in local pantomimes at Leusdon and Postbridge.

Tony Deeble.

Tom Cobley ⊕ TO WIDECOMBE FAIR *and all.*

With grey mare: Tom Pearse and Bill E   ver, Jan Stewer, Peter Gurney, Peter Davey, Dan'l Whiddon, Harry Hawke, old Uncle Tom Cobley...

Namesakes

During the research for this book we discovered three different Uncle Tom Cobley chairs, at Widecombe, Spreyton and Crediton.

Widecombe

Spreyton

Crediton

THE UNCLE TOM COBLEY NOVELTY RACE

The Uncle Tom Cobley Novelty Race first took place in 1931, when Mr Keith Fox of Natsworthy presented a Cup. The race has continued to the present day. The participants are transported to a point on the skyline at the top of Widecombe, between Bonehill Rocks and Tunhill Rocks and they have to find their own route back to the Fair field over rocks, bracken, gorse, bogs and having to cross the East Webburn river. Competitors are permitted to cross the road but cannot run down it. Local people have traditionally done very well in this event, winning on many occasions. Due to the rough terrain, competitors must be aged fourteen years or over.

The number of participants recorded in 1947 was eight, including (according to press reports) the first woman to take part. Present day competitors are more numerous, in the region of twenty-five.

In 1956 the Chairman of the Widecombe Fair Committee, General Sir Robert Sturgess who was connected with the Royal Marines at Lympstone, arranged for the provision of a Very Light which was fired from the top of the hill so that visitors to the Fair would know when the race had begun. For several years he brought a contingent of servicemen from Lympstone to take part and, from 1959 for many years, he presented a bottle of gin for the first serviceman home. This tradition has been maintained by the Committee to the present day. Despite the great number of armed service competitors taking part in the race over the years only once, in 1958 when Lieutenant Roderick Tuck won, has there been a service winner.

One competitor of note was Frank Nosworthy. Frank was a local boy having been born in Widecombe. He was the local postman and later in life became a farmer. He married Isobel Daw. His uncle was called Frank and so they became known as Big Frank and Little Frank.

Another successful local athlete was Bill Miners who competed regularly at Widecombe Fair from 1922-1933 winning many track and field events. They often trained together and Bill told Frank one day "You can beat me" so Frank decided to give the Uncle Tom Cobley race a go.

Frank was the winner of the Keith Fox Widecombe Fair Challenge Cup in the inaugural race of 1931 and for the next three years. He therefore won the cup outright. The Cup is now in the possession of his grandson Neil Nosworthy. Frank gave the other competitors a start by standing back ten paces but still managed to beat them to the finishing line. Keith Fox of Natsworthy kindly replaced the cup with a new perpetual trophy for the winner, which is still competed for today.

After World War II Frank was on the Widecombe Fair Committee and won prizes at the Fair when showing cart horses and sheep. After his death in 1976 his family donated a cup in his honour called the Frank Nosworthy Memorial Cup. It was to be presented to the first local runner home in the Uncle Tom Cobley Novelty Race.

In 1947 the race had its first woman competitor. She was Miss H. Barber of Plymouth. She came home some time after the rest of the field, limping and scratched, but undaunted by the experience. It was not thought she would try again. According to newspaper reports in 1948, local girl Jean Nosworthy, granddaughter of Edward Dunn the first Uncle Tom impersonator, took part at the age of sixteen and finished a very creditable fourth.

In 1965, when Bill Miners resigned from the committee, he offered a cup in memory of his years of service to the Fair. This was the W. F. Miners Perpetual Cup and was donated to the first lady home in the downhill race.

In 1972, the race was won by Colin Pearse with his twin brother, James, in second place, possibly the only time twins have achieved this feat.

Mrs R. H. Britton presents the prizes to the first three competitors to finish in the Uncle Tom Cobley Race in 1972. First was Colin Pearse (left), second his twin brother James and third Lloyd Mortimore (right)

In 1981, fifty years after the inauguration of the race and after having been the first woman home in 1978, 1979 and 1980, 19 year old bank clerk, Christine Slade of Isaford Farm became the first woman to win the race. This is the only time it has happened in the race's seventy five year history and, in doing so she won the Keith Fox Perpetual Challenge Cup as the winner, the Bill Miners' Perpetual Cup as the first woman home and the Frank Nosworthy Perpetual Challenge Cup as the first local runner home. The following year, 1982, she was again the first woman home achieving this feat for the fifth time in a row. She also won the Lady's Cup in 1984, making a total six times — a record!

A recent picture of Christine with the three cups she won in 1981.

Rhona Parker, a farmer's wife from Ashburton, also competed in 1982 and finished the downhill race for the first time since being the first woman home eighteen years earlier in 1964. She bet her husband £100 that she was fit enough to do it and proved her point.

Another notable achievement was in 2006, when Norah Lamb arrived at the finishing line hand in hand with her two daughters, Sharon Hutchins and Julie Elliot.

A special prize is given each year for the first veteran, aged 40 or over, to complete the race.

In the early 1990s a Junior Uncle Tom Cobley Race was inaugurated to encourage youngsters to participate. The course for children aged eight years and under is one lap of the Fairfield and the winner is presented with the Sue and Jayne Hutchings Perpetual Shield. Children aged nine years and over run two laps of the field, the winner being presented with the Smerdon Perpetual Challenge Shield.

UNCLE TOM COBLEY DOWNHILL NOVELTY RACE WINNERS

1931	Frank Nosworthy.	1971	Colin Pearse.
1932	Frank Nosworthy.	1972	Colin Pearse.
1933	Frank Nosworthy.	1973	Michael Vooght.
1934	Frank Nosworthy.	1974	Michael Vooght.
1935	E.Hurrell.	1975	Barry Knight.
1936	E.Hurrell.	1976	Barry Knight.
1937	P.Luxton.	1977	Barry Knight.
1938	J.F.White.	1978	David Ward.
1939-45	WWII.	1979	Barry Knight.
1945	Not run.	1980	Barry Knight.
1946	E.Prowse.	1981	Christine Slade .
1947	E.Prowse.	1982	Paul Hannaford.
1948	J.F.Newling.	1983	Paul Hext.
1949	Derek Hooper.	1984	Charles Mudge.
1950	John Goss.	1985	David Slade.
1951	John Swainson.	1986	David Slade.
1952	Derek Hooper.	1987	Geoffrey Partridge.
1953	R.Beckerlegge.	1988	David Ward.
1954	Derek Hooper.	1989	Geoffrey Partridge.
1955	F.Jeffery.	1990	Daniel Withers.
1956	F.Jeffery.	1991	Geoffrey Partridge.
1957	F.Jeffery.	1992	Geoffrey Partridge.
1958	Lt Roderick Tuck.	1993	Ben Deeble.
1959	Russell Pearse.	1994	Ben Deeble.
1960	Russell Pearse.	1995	Ben Deeble.
1961	Russell Pearse.	1996	Ben Deeble.
1962	Russell Pearse.	1997	Ben Deeble.
1963	John Vooght.	1998	Richard Osborne.
1964	John Vooght.	1999	Richard Osborne.
1965	John Vooght.	2000	Edward Lamb.
1966	Michael Lamb.	2001	Foot & Mouth.
1967	John Vooght.	2002	Sam Smerdon.
1968	John Vooght.	2003	Edward Lamb.
1969	Michael Vooght.	2004	Edward Lamb.
1970	Robin Giles.	2005	Edward Lamb.
		2006	Edward Lamb.

The statistics above were compiled from a combination of *Western Morning News, Mid Devon Advertiser* publications and Cup engravings.

EDEN PHILLPOTTS AND WIDECOMBE FAIR

Among the many writers who have tried to transfer the atmosphere of Dartmoor into print, Eden Phillpotts stands pre-eminent. He was born in India in 1862 while his father was an Officer in the Indian Army and a political agent. Eden was brought back to England by his mother and educated in Plymouth. It was at this early age that the seeds of his love of Dartmoor were sown.

He is probably best known locally for his *Dartmoor Cycle* series. This consists of eighteen novels and two books of short stories. Each novel is based in a different Dartmoor locality, full of colourful descriptions of people and places. Although he began writing in 1890, the first of the *Dartmoor Cycle - Children of the Mist* - based in Chagford, was not published until 1898.

Map of the locations of Eden Phillpotts Dartmoor Cycle Books

Widecombe Fair was Number fourteen in the series, published in 1913. One particular passage describing Fair Day in the early 1900s is full of local colour, which gradually succumbs to the climax of the day, in the shape of a grey and black thunderstorm creeping over Hameldown.

Eden Phillpotts's topographical detail is well matched with his use of old established local names. In *Widecombe Fair* we can find Coakers, Reeps and Smerdons, plus Messrs Cobleigh, Pierce, Gurney and Hawke. This latter quartet is another indication of the famous (or infamous) song. Just about every house in Widecombe at that time featured in the story, plus of course The Old Inn, the Rugglestone Inn and the Post Office. However, it must be pointed out that the characters with local names were all fictitious and not the actual occupiers of the properties mentioned..

Widecombe Fair was produced as a play on the London stage but with a change of title to *The Farmer's Wife*. The original script, consisting of 1098 handwritten pages, still exists in Plymouth Central Library.

In 1928, still under the title of *The Farmer's Wife*, it was made into a film. These were the days of black and white silent films with dramatic musical accompaniment. It was billed as a romantic comedy and had as its director the one and only Alfred Hitchcock. According to newspaper reports, it made headlines on 18th December 1928. *'Widecombe Fair – A fine British film* It received prolonged applause from a large audience at the London Hippodrome.' It was described as a charming semi-romantic comedy.

The Farmer's Wife (1928)

Directed by
Alfred Hitchcock

Writing credits
Eden Phillpotts (play)
Eliot Stannard (adaptation)

Eden Phillpotts died in 1960, his ashes scattered on Dartmoor. He left behind seventy years of almost continuous writing. In his prime, he was producing two or three books a year. These covered a very wide range, including plays, novels, poetry, children's stories and gardening. It is in his *Dartmoor Cycle* that he produced such feelings for this part of Devon, a landscape of labour and love.

This chapter has been compiled with information and assistance from another author and lover of Dartmoor, Kenneth F. Day.

CUPS AND TROPHIES

HORSE/PONY CLASSES

Simmons Perpetual Challenge Cup - Best Dartmoor Pony.
Kent Memorial Perpetual Challenge Cup - Best Dartmoor Opposite Sex.
Geraldine May Perpetual Challenge Cup - Best Dartmoor Pony Under three years.
Shilston Rocks Perpetual Challenge Trophy - Best Dartmoor Filly.
Lady Edith Brooke Perpetual Challenge Cup - Best Registered Dartmoor.
Miss M. Hamlyn Perpetual Silver Salver - Most points in the Dartmoor Classes.
Bincombe Challenge Cup - Best Shetland Male.
Luckdon Perpetual Challenge Cup - Best Shetland Mare.
W. W. Whitley Perpetual Challenge Cup - Best Shetland Pony under three years.
The Routley Shield – Best Veteran.

Some of the Trophies donated over the years

Flamingo Perpetual Shield & Champagne - Best Cob.
David Parnell Memorial Perpetual Challenge Cup - Best local Cob.
Barker-Schofield Perpetual Challenge Cup- Best Mountain & Moorland.
J. H. Hine Perpetual Challenge Cup – Best Arab.
Newton Abott Rural District Council Perpetual Challenge Cup – Best Brood Mare.
Shillibeer Lakehead Perpetual Challenge Cup - Best Shetland Foal.
Beinkowska Perpetual Challenge Cup - Best Yearling in the one, two or three year old Class.

Beinkowska Perpetual Challenge Cup - Best 2-3 year old.
Miss Pen-Gaskell Scobitor Perpetual Challenge Cup – Best Hunter.
Kirsty Peake Perpetual Challenge Cup - Best Local Hunter.
Widecombe Fair Perpetual Challenge Cup - Winner of the Lead Rein class.
Herbie Perpetual Trophy - Winner Local Lead Rein class.
Widecombe Fair Perpetual Challenge Cup - Winner Child's Pony, 14.2.
Tiddy Perpetual Challenge Cup - Best pony ridden by child 12 and under.
Widecombe Fair Bill Brewer Perpetual Challenge Cup - Best Child's Pony/Horse.
Foxworthy Trophy - Local Most Suitable Pony/Horse - Child Under 16 Years.
S. G. Harris Cup - Local Most Suitable Pony/Horse - Best exhibit aged 11 or under.

SHEEP CLASSES
C. Mortimore Perpetual Challenge Cup - Most points in Greyfaced Dartmoors.
Ned Northmore Perpetual Memorial Trophy - Champion Whitefaced Dartmoors.
Mann Bros. Perpetual Challenge Cup - Best Whitefaced Dartmoor Ram.
C. W. Abel Perpetual Challenge Cup - Best exhibit, Whitefaced Dartmoor flock under 80.
P. W. Coaker Perpetual Challenge Cup - Best Pen local Whitefaced Dartmoors.
F. A. Mortimore Perpetual Challenge Cup - Most points Local Sheep.
South West Farmers Perpetual Challenge Cup - Best local Ram.
S. Trant Perpetual Memorial Cup - Most points in Local Classes.

GYMKHANA
Widecombe Fair Perpetual Challenge Cup – Most points in Gymkhana Lead Rein Classes.
Blue Grass Perpetual Challenge Cup - Most points in the other Gymkhana Classes.

OTHER
British Legion Perpetual Challenge Cup - Most points, Children's Handicrafts.
Hermon French Perpetual Challenge Salver - Most points Vegetable, Plant & Flower Classes.
Widecombe Fair Perpetual Challenge Rose Bowl - Most points, Produce and Handicrafts.
Joan Perkins Memorial Perpetual Challenge Cup - Best Local Vegetable.
Widecombe Fair Tame Perpetual Challenge Cup - Exhibitor aged 7 years and under gaining the most points in the Home Produce Classes.

FANCY DRESS
Widecombe Fair Perpetual Challenge Cup - Winner Mounted Fancy Dress.
Partridge Perpetual Challenge Cup - Winner Unmounted Fancy Dress.

UNCLE TOM COBLEY RACES
Keith Fox Perpetual Challenge Cup - Winner.
W. F. Miners Perpetual Challenge Cup - First Lady.
F. Nosworthy Memorial Perpetual Challenge Cup - First Local.

CHILDREN'S UNCLE TOM COBLEY RACE
Sue & Jayne Hutchings Perpetual Shield - aged 8yrs or under.
Smerdon Perpetual Challenge Shield - aged 9yrs or over.

BALE TOSSING
The Partridge Family Perpetual Challenge Cup for the first Gentleman.
Perpetual Challenge Cup for the first Lady.

TUG OF WAR
E. Avery Perpetual Challenge Cup - Best Local Team.
Kitson Perpetual Challenge Cup - Open.

Official Programme   *Price Three Pence*

WIDECOMBE FAIR

TUESDAY, SEPT. 14th, 1937

ADMISSION TO THE FIELD 1/-

OFFICIALS

President and Chairman	...... P. P. WHITLEY, Esq.
Hon. Secretary	...... W. SATTERLEY
Agricultural Secretary	...... J. HINE.
Treasurer	...... T. DAW.

JUDGES

Sheep	Mr. F. R. COAKER, Sherberton
Ponies	Mr. H. Madders, South Zeal.

" Advertiser " Typs., Newton Abbot